Praise for *Separated by* ~~Duty, United in Love~~

"The most important book military ~~f~~
—Gene~~ral~~
Air C~~orps~~

"Your mother couldn't have told you better! Honest, sage advice from someone who has truly been there, done that ... from both sides of the separation. Should be required reading for military spouses. You'll find yourself saying, 'Whew, so this is normal!' at every page."
                    —**Sarah Smiley,** syndicated columnist and author of *Going Overboard: The Misadventures of a Military Wife*

"Well-written and -conceived, something of value not just to military couples but everyone in a relationship trying to balance family and career."   —**Mark Bowden,** author of *Black Hawk Down*

"*Separated by Duty, United in Love* is an essential handbook for military families. Shellie Vandevoorde demystifies the deployment process and passes on valuable advice from the 'trenches,' military families who have successfully endured and grown closer despite their separation."
—**Sara Rosett,** author of *Moving Is Murder,* A Mom Zone Mystery

"A must-read for everyone in or associated with the military! A well-organized, thought-provoking, insightful guide for the everyday 'living apart' that each member of the military is subject to. I enjoyed your book so much I could not put it down until finished."
                    —Brigadier General **Dennis Leadbetter,** USAF (Ret.)

"What I learned in twenty-five years with the Marine Corps—the hard way—is in this book. *Separated by Duty, United in Love* is a frank and truly practical manual of everything you need to know about keeping marriage, family and your sanity strong through military life. Valuable, time tested, and a much-needed resource for new and not-so-new military couples."
                    —**Amy J. Fetzer,** Marine wife and author of *Perfect Weapon*

"This is a clearly written, practical guide to coping with separation that should be required reading for military spouses."
—Colonel **Michael B. Dayoub,** D.D.S., M.S., U.S. Army (Ret.)

"I wish I had your book during my eleven years of military experience. I think it would have saved me a lot of heartache. For those seeking more than the socials or meetings that the military offers to get through emotional and trying times."
—Staff Sergeant **Waynette Spinzig,** U.S. Army (veteran)

"I feel that if military wives had access to your book, it could provide them with *real* practical advice for handling deployments. Your book could easily be that desperately needed ounce of prevention that military wives need."
—**Maggie,** "Active duty mental health care provider and wife of active duty soldier"

CITADEL PRESS BOOKS are published by

Kensington Publishing Corp.
119 West 40th Street
New York, NY 10018

All Kensington titles, imprints, and distributed lines are available at special
quantity discounts for bulk purchases for sales promotions, premiums,
fund-raising, educational, or institutional use. Special book excerpts or
customized printings can also be created to fit specific needs. For details,
write or phone the office of the Kensington special sales manager:
Kensington Publishing Corp., 119 West 40th Street, New York, NY 10018,
attn: Special Sales Department; phone 1-800-221-2647.

First printing: March 2006
First printing (updated edition): May 2010

10 9 8 7 6 5 4 3 2 1

Printed in the United States of America

Library of Congress Control Number: 2005934016

ISBN-13: 978-0-8065-3199-1
ISBN-10: 0-8065-3199-1

SEPARATED BY DUTY, UNITED IN LOVE

A Guide to Long-Distance Relationships for Military Couples

NEW UPDATED EDITION

Shellie Vandevoorde

CITADEL PRESS
Kensington Publishing Corp
www.kensingtonbooks.com

THIS BOOK is dedicated to all the brave, wonderful, military families and the sacrifices they make every day; to all my friends, men and women, who offered their insights which make this book what it is, especially Deborrah Cisneros, Kelli McMorris, Carol Herrick, and the Hooah Chaplain "S"; to my editor Michaela Hamilton, and copy editors Bonnie Fredman and Holly Fairbank, for their expertise and needed guidance; to my wonderful family for always supporting me; and to my God who inspires me.

CONTENTS

WHY I WROTE THIS BOOK

AS AN ARMY VETERAN, former law enforcement officer, military spouse, and mother fine-tuning my way through military life, learning more and more as the years and the deployments go by, I have heard couples in all branches of the military bring up the same concerns repeatedly.

Robin, a military spouse: "The kids are having such a hard time this deployment, I don't know what to do!"

Me: "Why don't you go to the PX [post exchange] or Military Clothing and Sales stores where I'm sure you will find a book dealing with all these issues."

A few days later:

Robin: "There aren't any books anywhere."

Me: "I find that hard to believe. Are you sure you looked everywhere, even at the Military Clothing and Sales store? That store usually has a lot of military-specific books."

I didn't believe Robin, so I drove to the post and looked for myself. Sure enough, I didn't see one book dealing with relationship issues for the military couple! Later I was telling my brother, Chuck, about this problem, and he simply told me, "Why don't you write the book?"

The seed had been planted. Perhaps I could provide a book as a guide for couples (married and unmarried) of all ages and all branches of the military. The information would help newly-weds and long-married couples, where either the husband or the wife or both are in the service or either spouse may be away on a deployment or one may be a stay-at-home spouse. You will find something for whatever category you are in, with the roles changing at different times. I would like to help these couples deal with our unique way of life, especially during deployments. After all, I was currently working as a detective. Thus, I told myself I would do a little investigating on how and why some military couples make it and some do not. I would conduct de-tailed interviews with those who have successful military mar-riages and then put everyone's experience and solutions together in my own little case study!

The title of my first self-published edition was *How to Survive a Long-Distance Relationship*. It has received some great re-views, and readers have requested more details and offered helpful comments. In this new edition, I have added new topics and expanded on some old ones. I have continued to seek the input from happy, successful, and strong military couples. Whether you are a newlywed or have been married a long time and you are in the Army, Air Force, Navy, Marines, Coast Guard, National Guard, or Reserves, I hope that you will benefit from the lessons of those of us who have walked your path. May you gain comfort, understanding, and strength through this book.

INTRODUCTION

WHEN OUR SERVICE MEMBER is home and life is happy, it's easy to enjoy the military lifestyle. However, when duty calls, many of us decide this isn't the life for us anymore. When training exercises or real world deployments or both take our service member away from home, some of us complain so much that our loved one doesn't want to call home when he or she finally does get the opportunity. We may display our anger to our service members after days or weeks of not hearing from them. We may even tell him or her how fed up we are and issue an ultimatum: it's either the job or us.

It takes two to make a happy marriage, but when we marry a service member, we have to understand that life will not be easy and that we will be apart because of training exercises, deployments, school, and so on. Furthermore, we need to understand these things are out of our service member's control.

Separations are the times that will make or break your marriage. They are the times when you will be asked to be "the selfless giver." Your service member may ask you to sacrifice your career, schooling, or friends, and being close to family— the list could go on. Mostly, you will be asked to give of yourself, and your time. As a military spouse, you will make these sacrifices as your part in supporting your service member's patriotism, courage, and commitment to something he or she believes in.

Your commitment to stand by your service member and keep the home fires burning is not always easy to keep. This commitment sets military spouses apart. We will have to make sacrifices that may seem unfair at times, and we may feel like we

For service members who are reading this book, if you want a spouse or partner committed to your decision to be a warrior in the fight for freedom and liberty, you need to do these three things:

1. Include your spouse in all decisions and changes that affect the family. Discuss your military goals with your spouse.

2. Make family decisions that you both agree on. I know of spouses who don't have a clue as to what their service member does on a daily basis or what their service member's career goals may be. Some spouses have told me their service members don't want them to be involved in support groups or have anything to do with the unit he or she is assigned to. You as a service member need to know that support groups, involvement in the unit and with other military spouses will help your spouse "get by" during times of separation. Service members who decide to keep their spouses "in the dark" about important decisions and "shelter them from the unit" make it very hard, if not impossible, for their loved ones to remain committed to a military marriage and way of life.

3. Most important, make the most of every opportunity that you have to be together as a family. Reconsider separations when other options are available. It may not seem like the best or easiest option for a spouse to lose a job or postpone a degree because of relocation, but sometimes family must be your number one priority. Being at war has taught us all how short and precious time is.

are the ones doing all the giving. However, as a military spouse you are and will forever be "the wind beneath their wings." Some of us will face hard times, challenges beyond our belief, but those who stay the course become the "rock" of the family.

If you have chosen to be a military spouse, you will face many challenges ahead. Some days these challenges will seem like mountains. By surrounding yourself with others who have made the same commitment to stand by their service member, you will never be alone and you will always have help climbing that mountain.

Chapter 1

DEPARTURE AND THE GAMES WE PLAY

I DON'T KNOW HOW to ease the pain of the moment of departure, but you can take comfort in knowing that each deployment can bring you closer, even when you are apart. You and your loved one must decide, and commit to, which way to grow. Many relationships never make it through this test of time, but the ones that do become extra special and much deeper than we could ever imagine. Some of us are struggling and will continue to struggle through this process, and I can only hope some of the ideas in this book will help you through those rough times.

Put your trust in what other couples have been through. I have attempted to choose the most well-balanced, loving, experienced relationships I could find and put their suggestions and real-life experiences in this book. The solutions you are reading are time tested. They work!

STAGE 1: THE MIND GAMES
(PRIOR TO SEPARATION/DEPLOYMENT)

The "I'd rather be angry than hurt" game

Every time my husband walked down the passageway or out to the flight line to get on the plane for a deployment, I would go through mixed senses of guilt, shame, sadness, and misery. I often wondered, why did these past weeks have to be so hard? Can I spend the next twenty-plus years (the usual time of a military career) going through this?

It took me a long time to realize why anger, tension, and other not-so-loving feelings toward each other grew in the days leading up to his departure. They would usually begin about one to two weeks prior to his leaving. We disagreed a lot, and it seemed that little things would set us off. We would finally reach a point that I call the "just leave and get it over with" attitude.

I've talked with many couples, both military and civilian, who have encountered the same feelings and have experienced the same general stages without understanding why. I think this process is the heart's defense mechanism taking over. It is your mind's way of trying to ease the pain of your loved one leaving. Longer absences tend to bring on more of this game playing.

Time and time again I have regretted this predeployment hardening of my heart. After all these mind games I found myself just as miserable—and worse, I had to deal with guilt for some of my behavior. My thoughts would run wild, and I would find myself on an emotional roller coaster.

Ana's story

"I knew I was transferring the anger I felt about Joe's deployment and our separation onto him. I felt like my husband was going on a vacation from the responsibilities of raising the kids, keeping the house, and paying the bills as well as everything in between. Without him my life became more difficult, and I felt overwhelmed."

My own defensive behavior finally dawned on me when we were preparing to move back to the United States after being stationed in Italy for three years. We had met some wonderful friends while we were there, and I noticed that the closer we got to our moving date, the more distant our families became. I realized then that even our families were playing a game to lessen the pain of the separation from dear friends. I looked back and understood I had played the same game when I left home to join the army many years prior.

It all began to make sense to me. I also realized my husband and I played this same game with each deployment. The game may lessen the pain for the moment, but in the end we suffer more from the guilty feelings we are left with. It may be months or even over a year before we see our loved one, or many years may pass before we see some of our long-distance friends. Now is not the time to be playing this game.

Sadly, several friends have told me they never play this game because they never talk about their service member leaving. Talk about a communication breakdown! After the service member has left, the spouse often feels bad that important conversations never occurred.

The only way my husband and I stopped going through this stage was to recognize it and admit (not easy) what we were doing. It took us a long time to realize when we were game playing and longer to own up to it. This game is one of the most common, but it leaves you feeling awful during your time apart. Stop it while you can and you will not be sorry later.

The "I've got to love you while I can" game

I feel this is the better of the many games we play. However, it, too, can lead to the "just leave" attitude. In this game, we excessively show our love before our partners leave. We do this in a number of ways, and the time frame remains the same (about one to two weeks prior to departure).

More men than women have told me about this game. Here are some of their comments:

★ "She starts wanting to hold my hand in public or walk with our arms around each other more than normal."

★ "She seems so clingy."

★ "She follows me around the house while I'm trying to pack and wants to talk about our whole life."

★ "She tells me she loves me one hundred times a day."

★ Dave told me, "It's not that guys don't love the extra attention, but after two weeks of this, I'm ready to leave!"

On the other hand, women have different grievances:

★ "He's so preoccupied I can't talk with him about important issues."

★ "All he wants is sex, sex, sex."

★ "He buys me little gifts we can't really afford."

★ A few women have even told me that their boyfriends have proposed just before a yearlong hardship tour to Korea or combat. It's not that wives and girlfriends don't adore the additional caring, but they realize that most often it's just a deployment/separation thing, and they frequently wonder, "Why can't he be like this all the time?"

This game is easy to recognize, and most of the time I don't even bring it to my husband's attention. I feel it is the most rewarding and enjoyable of all the games we play, and I look back on it fondly after he leaves. The drawback of this game is the sudden loss of all the extra love and affection. If you play this game—and I encourage you to try it—it really plays on your heart when your loved one is gone, but in a great way.

After several years of frequent deployments, I feel better with this game than any of the other ones I play. I never have guilty feelings to contend with. My heart aches at times and I know I set myself up for the love withdrawal, but after playing the "I'd rather be mad than hurt" game for many years, this one is a welcome change.

The only way to stop the "I've got to love you while I can" game (if you must) is to try to act and feel as normal as possible. Keep your daily routine the same before and after the deployment. Remember, the longer the separation, the more we play these games. Thus, the more heartache we feel.

One friend, Tonya, reported that she and her husband spent as much quality time together as possible. Another friend, Vivian, said she and her husband first played the "I'd rather be angry than hurt game," and then they switched to the "I've got to love you while I can" game a day or two before a deployment.

The "professional" game

I'm sure a lot of us have been through this one. The whole deployment becomes a checklist, and we deal with everything in a cold, professional manner. The real issues of love, stress, and anxiety you push to the back burner and they never come up, or they seem inappropriate due to time or circumstance. Organized people like this game, and to them, the separation is just another organizational challenge. Or rather, it feels that way to the loved one on the receiving end.

My friend Sherry has been married to a service member for over fifteen years, so I asked her to share what kind of games they play. Sadly, she related, "We fight for about three or four days before he leaves." Sherry added, "I also get the famous Safety

Briefing. You know, don't forget to lock the doors, don't leave the dogs outside when neighbor kids are in the yard, don't forget where the gun is." She told me she knows all this and the warnings are just common sense, but she listens to him each time just for the fun of it.

If you are going too far into the organizational, work-related mode, tackle it head on and go to a different level. Deal with the issues at hand that either one or both of you want, or need, to talk about. When your spouse is gone, it will never seem like the right time to discuss these matters, and you will regret that you didn't take advantage of the time you had together before the departure.

The "telling the kids" game

This is never a fun game to play. I have discovered for myself and many have told me that the more time a child has to adjust to a parent's deployment and separation, the better things will go. Good advice came from Mary, who has young children. She told me her strategy was to "tell them about two weeks in advance and then remind them of it as the day got closer." In the past we would wait till the last few days before telling our then young son about Dad's upcoming deployment. We thought that he really didn't understand time as we do, so we were doing him a favor. Looking back, I feel we were wrong.

About five months before my husband was to depart for a yearlong "hardship tour," in Korea, our five-year-old son accidentally overheard us discussing the matter. When he confronted us, we had no choice but to tell him the truth. This turned out to be a blessing in disguise. Our son came up with plenty of questions over the next five months that, thankfully, his dad was there to help answer. More important, my husband took an active part in discussing all the fears our son was having and was able to comfort him in a way only a father can. Dad lifted a big burden from me when he was able to help with the conversations about those fears and ease the mood swings our son seemed to go through. Our son understood his dad's leaving much better than he had in the past. On departure day, despite the tears, it went better than I had hoped.

Maria's advice

"Deal with the children in a way that will cause as little stress as possible. Some kids are cool with anything; some freak out over every little thing. You are the only ones who really know your child. Don't let family and friends tell you what is best. You two make the decision.

"Try to include them in whatever you are doing, and let them know of the ways that they can communicate with Dad or Mom, such as letters, pictures, and e-mail. Always be honest with them."

Ready for the roller coaster? The departure

Now that you're physically and emotionally drained, the big day you've dreaded—Departure Day (D-Day)—has arrived. You know that feelings of loneliness, stress, anxiety, and overwhelming responsibility will hit you. This anticipation tends to put a damper on your good-byes. Your mouth gets dry, you feel a lump in your throat, and you realize few words exist at this point. What you needed to say should have already been said because now you are feeling too many emotions to concentrate on anything but the moment at hand.

At this time, you should try to control your thoughts. I've found myself wondering, "Is this the last time we'll see each other?" or "Will things be the same when he returns?" Tammy told me, "You must remind yourself that it's not forever." We tend to "what if" the situation repeatedly and usually think of the worst-case scenarios. Stop, stop, stop! No way can you predict what the future will hold, and by allowing your mind to play "what if," you will drive yourself into a state of depression. You can't change a thing, and as hard as it may be, we can't worry about what we can't change. Take a deep breath, and start planning meaningful activities that will keep you and your mind busy. Dwell on positive thoughts (as hard as they may seem to come by).

I've learned over the years that what I call the "deployment site to Wal-Mart routine" can be helpful for the kids as well as me. When your loved one leaves, take the children out of the house and go anywhere to buy a little something or just go somewhere besides back to a quiet house. This outing doesn't have to cost much, and it's an effective diversion for the first day, which I find, is one of the hardest. Most of us want to go home and isolate ourselves for a while, but being alone just makes things worse. The kids can feel your anxiety, so a little field trip is good for everybody.

STAGE 2: DEPRESSION (0–2 WEEKS)

Now that he or she has just left, loneliness, sadness, boredom, anxiety, and all the other awful departure-day emotions set in, and it seems no one is there to talk with about it. Nothing really sounds good to do, or you just want to be alone. Those who have departed have either a mission or business to concentrate on, while the rest of us have to stay home to deal with the kids and all the other responsibilities of the home front. The prospect can be overwhelming. You can sit and feel sorry about your situation and wish things were another way because that's the easy way. But feeling sorry for yourself isn't going to help.

The best plan for the first two weeks is to have a full schedule. Do not allow yourself time to sit and dwell on your emotions at this crucial time.

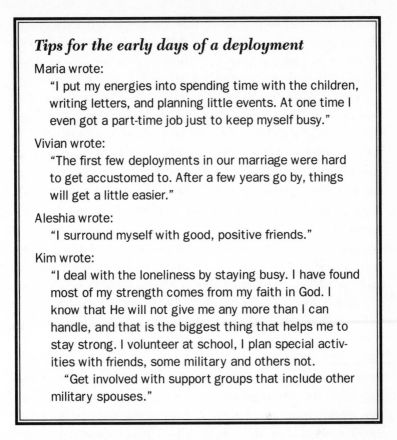

Tips for the early days of a deployment

Maria wrote:

"I put my energies into spending time with the children, writing letters, and planning little events. At one time I even got a part-time job just to keep myself busy."

Vivian wrote:

"The first few deployments in our marriage were hard to get accustomed to. After a few years go by, things will get a little easier."

Aleshia wrote:

"I surround myself with good, positive friends."

Kim wrote:

"I deal with the loneliness by staying busy. I have found most of my strength comes from my faith in God. I know that He will not give me any more than I can handle, and that is the biggest thing that helps me to stay strong. I volunteer at school, I plan special activities with friends, some military and others not.

"Get involved with support groups that include other military spouses."

I asked my friend Kim (an Army Special Forces wife) how she copes with all the frequent deployments. She simply said, "I never let myself feel sorry for myself, I'm afraid if I do I won't be able to stand it."

I know firsthand, it's easy to think, "If only Grandma and Grandpa were here to help with the kids," or "If only I lived closer to home, I could visit more," or "If only I had a best friend close by." We find ourselves wanting what we don't have. I'm here to tell you, if you seek out friendships, participate in meaningful activities, and get involved with support groups, church groups, and self-help classes, that most military installations offer for free, many if not all your needs will be met. No, they're not your grandma or your best friend, but other relationships will develop and become very meaningful.

This is a good time to listen to the complaints of your civilian friends. I challenge you to listen, really listen. You will eventually hear one of them wishing his or her spouse would go on a deployment for a while! You may also hear them complaining about the in-laws coming over again. If you tune in your ears and listen, you will soon realize that all the things you think will make you feel better could in fact make you miserable in a different way.

I'm all for being around family and the support they offer, especially during a deployment. Many times I have wished I could just pack up, go home, and forget about military life for a while. I know all too well, this will not solve my problems, just relocate them.

I've talked with a number of spouses who decided to move back home during deployments. Many regretted it. They tell me their families were loving and supportive, but really didn't understand what they were going through. These spouses were also out of the information loop that's so valuable while our service members are away. If we live across the country from our families, many of us can't afford to buy a plane ticket to go home for every deployment, and if we're overseas, we're lucky to visit relatives once a year.

Keep in mind that in just about two short weeks you will feel completely different. I am not saying you are going to stop feeling lonely, but when you have a week or two behind you, it is much easier to deal with your separation. If we are honest with ourselves, many of us have realized that through each deployment we have become stronger, more independent individuals. Few welcome this challenge, but once accomplished, you will one day realize that during difficult times, your love grows to much deeper levels.

What happens when after two weeks or more we don't feel better? What happens when we know we're not adjusting and we can't seem to find a new routine? We must learn to be honest with ourselves. For the sake of our entire family and our children, there is a time when we may need to seek professional help. I'm not a medical professional but I have talked with one, and she advised me that if we go for a period of time and can't find sleep, if we never leave our house or get off the couch or out of the bed, if our mood and feelings affect our going to work or sending the kids to school, or caring for them, then it may be time to call a professional. I honestly feel we will know in our heart of hearts if we are lonely or if something more is going on.

Kelli advised:

"If your friends, especially those whose opinions you respect, tell you that counseling or 'a doctor's consultation is something that might be beneficial,' or you hear, 'We are worried about you,' or 'You have not been yourself for some time,' or worse yet, your children ask, 'Why are you grumpy/[or sad] all the time, Mommy?' it may be time to seek help."

If you are "the friend," don't hesitate to make your observations known to your friend. Many times we avoid recognizing the symptoms ourselves. Unit Chaplains are a great source of help because, first and foremost, everything is confidential. Second, they can provide a sense of hope. Many times that is all we need.

Oh, by the way, some of the top stressors in life are moving, marital separation, pregnancy, finances, death (family or friends), changing jobs, taking a mortgage, foreclosure, major change in responsibilities, changing schools (kids), and change in sleeping habits. Hello . . . does this sound like everyday military life at its best? Do not think for one minute you are weak if you feel a little overwhelmed. This is why military families are special and not everyone would or could put up with this way of life.

Military OneSource (www.militaryonesource.com) has recently increased its number of face-to-face counseling visits for each issue for all service members and families. All we have to do is contact them. We will always receive trained professionals online 24/7 and they will assist us in finding a provider in our local area or even outside our local area if we prefer. None of the counseling is ever reported to our service member's unit (as with everything, a few exceptions apply), and best of all, it's *free*.

I know many spouses who have sought professional counseling and swear by it. Many have also taken their children. It has made all the difference in the world. There is no shame in trying to help yourself or your children adapt to the many challenges life throws at us. Take advantage of the opportunities available to us as military members. Many civilians wish they had a chance to have the counseling options we have for our families for themselves or their children.

Sleep disorders

> For the first few days of deployment, Lu told me she literally goes for days without much sleep and waits till exhaustion takes over.

Most everyone I've talked with has reported difficulty sleeping when a loved one is away, especially during combat missions. Seven sleep tips from the pros are:

1. Make sure that the hour or two before bedtime is a wind-down period. Try to do something relaxing or nontaxing mentally. For instance, don't watch the local news with its twenty-four-hour coverage or any overexciting shows, don't pay bills, don't read scary books, and don't play intense video games or engage in any activity that gets you worked up either physically or mentally.

2. Start a relaxing bedtime routine as suggested by one friend. She takes her shower, gets the kids to bed, and reads her Bible or a positive self-help book before bed.

3. Take an occasional over-the-counter sleep aid, but if you have children in the house, keep such medication in a safe place.

4. Follow what some spouses have told me they do. Have a glass of wine, take a bubble bath, and enjoy an easy-read magazine or listen to soft, slow music, all of which are relaxing.

5. Control any negative thoughts that enter your mind, and replace them with positive images and goals or dreams. Dwell on "truth" not "what ifs."

6. Consider the advice in one magazine that reported jasmine-scented rooms could decrease anxiety.

7. Make your room dark to help you fall asleep faster and stay asleep longer. A sleep mask helps.

You *must* invest in a body pillow. You will enjoy wrapping your body around it, hugging it all night long. My #1 Favorite Sleep Aid.

How long the depression lasts will often depend on your mind control. If you allow your thoughts to run wild, you will feel every negative emotion to its fullest. Remember, you must control your thoughts or they will control you. I've read some wonderful books on this subject, and they all say the number one choice we all have is to "control our thoughts." Some of these titles are listed in the resource section at the end of this book.

Train your mind to think pleasing, kind, peaceful thoughts, and your outlook and attitude will be positive and encouraging. On the other hand, if you fill your mind, thoughts, and conversations with negative, depressing, and untrue statements, of course you will feel fear and unnecessary anxiety.

Staying focused on the positive is a lot harder than you may think. I challenge you to try it for a complete twenty-four hours. Observe how many times negative thoughts pop into your mind or worse, out your lips! If you can make it for twenty-four hours, try it for a whole week and see what happens. What do you have to lose—a pity party, a frowning face, mood swings, or wild thoughts that control your every minute? Life is too short to spend your precious time in this stage, let's move on.

STAGE 3: THE RESENTMENT

Although I tell myself I don't want to feel this way with each deployment, somehow at some time resentment creeps in. It usually happens after the depression stage, but it may come and go at any time. I know that my loved one can't help being away most of the time, but somehow it does matter to me when I'm left behind. I'm feeling lonely, sometimes bored, and the responsibilities of taking care of our child, the house, the vehicles, the pets, the work schedule, the bills, and everything else can spark resentment. Sometimes the resentment starts out slowly, but it grows with each new and difficult situation.

Kim's story

"Resentment does rear its ugly head every once in a while—usually when something has broken or gone wrong and it is my responsibility to handle it by myself or when the kids have gotten on my nerves after a long day and no one is there to take over. I have to remind myself that my husband can't do anything about this situation; therefore I can't blame him when things aren't easy. I have to tell myself again, I knew he would be away from home during his military career, and now is the time to be strong and make things work."

One way to get through this resentment stage is to remind yourself that your loved one appreciates what you are doing while he or she is away. To avoid having your loved one reach this stage, service members must let their spouses know as often as possible how much they appreciate them.

Seven ways for a service member to show appreciation during deployments or a long training exercise

1. Tell your spouse how much you appreciate what she or he does while you are away, repeatedly, and mean it.

2. Send a mushy, romantic card. (Carlos's special)

3. Hide little gifts around the house or bedroom, before leaving on a deployment and periodically tell your spouse where to find one of the gifts. (Jake's way of showing appreciation)

4. Let your spouse know you miss home, not just fast food or Starbucks.

5. Request photos of your spouse, not your dog.

6. Send flowers for no special occasion, except to say "Thanks." (A wife whose husband didn't make it back received flowers the day before he was killed. They were a true gift she will never forget. Corey's gift)

7. Make arrangements with one of your spouse's "same sex" friends and have the friend take your spouse out to dinner or a movie for you.

Lena told me that when she and her loved one are apart, "he takes stock in romantic cards. I get at least one a week. He will also send money to a friend of mine and have her go buy a rose and put it on my doorstep to let me know how much he loves me." Now tell me, how long could you feel resentful after receiving a rose on your doorstep? I hope many service members will read this and take heed!

A friend named Wanda told me, "He wrote often and would send little gifts to the kids and me. Once, from Vietnam, he sent a box of candy for the kids and in the center of the candy was a beautiful ring for me."

Anger and stress

I don't always feel that I should share my anger and stress with my loved one because venting these emotions can cause a communication breakdown—unless we have total confidence in knowing where each other is coming from, which is rare.

I was once telling my husband about an especially stressful

week, and even before we hung up the phone, I was mad at him. I could feel the tension over the line. I hadn't planned our conversation this way, and I didn't start out mad at him. When I hung up, I wondered, "How did that happen?"

The next day I told my girlfriend Robin about the situation:

Me: "Can you believe my husband seemed mad after I told him about my week from hell?"

Robin: "Did you tell him that you weren't blaming him for your stress, but that you were just telling him so you could vent?"

Me: "I think he should already know that I wasn't blaming him, and I don't see why he would think it was his fault anyway."

Me to husband next time he called: "Hey hon, during our last conversation, you know that I was not in any way blaming you for all my stress, and that I was just talking to you about it because you're my best friend, right?"

Husband: "I'm glad you told me that, because I felt you were blaming me."

I wondered how many times I had done the same thing without explaining to him that I knew it was not his fault—that I just needed to tell someone who understands me. Often those of us in a military marriage, especially young marriages, do not have close friends on hand whom we can talk with or loved ones with whom we can share our frustrations, even when they are on deployment. That kind of talk can backfire and cause more problems than if we had not said anything. Talk about a catch-22!

> One night my girlfriend Robin and I were discussing the resentment stage at length, and just for fun and confirmation we called Ann, whose husband had been on deployment for about two and a half weeks.
>
> Robin: "Hey, Ann, how's it going?"
> Ann: "Fine, I guess."
> Robin: "I'm over here at Shellie's house, and we are talking about the book she's writing. We just want to know how you feel toward your husband right now?"
> Ann: "I hate him right now!"

We all laughed because we knew exactly what she was going through—Resentment Stage! Our conversation confirmed how drastic our emotions could get during a deployment. Resentment can be hard to overcome, especially when your loved one may be on a fun training exercise, staying in a hotel, eating out with the gang every night, and having a ball while we're back home feeling miserable. This doesn't occur often, but when it does, service members need to beware that your left-behind spouse may be a bit resentful.

Shannon, another friend, told me that she feels resentment is natural, but if you feel that way the whole time, then there is a problem.

Why do I have to carry all the weight?

I've asked myself this question a thousand times, and I believe I may have found the answer. When we are left behind during a deployment, we are the ones who always have to carry out the "business as usual." Sometimes this means a large increase in responsibility. We must learn to take one day at a time and control our thoughts, never dwell on what we may have to face, and learn, most of all, to find enjoyment in each day. Treat yourself to something small like a relaxing bath or, even better, a motivational talk with a friend who's been there and understands exactly where you may be at that moment.

We can take any situation in life and think of it in a positive manner or negative manner. I can go for weeks with negative feelings before I realize what I'm doing. A little trick for coping is to be sure whatever you say, only speak the positive. Only let nice things come from your lips. You will soon notice how hard this can be. If you listen closely to those around you, more often you will hear people speaking of the negative things in life. That is all we seem to be interested in.

> I was at a Pampered Chef party with all military spouses except one civilian woman. Somehow the conversation turned into everyone complaining about the commissary, medical treatment, etc. Later I felt embarrassed and ungrateful, especially because our civilian guest said nothing.

Try it for a day, and take note of how many times you had to stop yourself from saying something negative. Looking for the good in everything gets me some curious looks, but since so much can be gained from a positive attitude, it's well worth it.

Of course, I don't mean you should never talk about your predicament with anyone. I have often kept my own feelings and frustrations to myself, and it never helps. When I can talk to a friend I trust, I always feel better. However, sometimes it's hard to find a trusting friendship or your best friend is busy with his or her life, and you don't want to be a burden.

When we find ourselves in a new location, having left our good friends behind, we must learn to become more proactive in seeking out friendships. Don't allow a few letdowns stop you from making new friends. Remember to be a good friend is to be a good listener.

Pat advises, "Surround yourself with the military community. Living on a base can be very helpful, because everyone there knows what you are going through." You are not the only one going through stressful times, lonely times, and hair-pulling times. We are in this together. Many of us have different experiences we can share to help others get through tough times, but how you choose to deal with your situation is up to you. Get involved and seek help if you need it.

Judy's story

"Time is a great healer for many things. Sometimes my feelings get better with time, but on a long deployment, my feelings change with circumstances, like a child's birthday, a special performance at sports or church, things that draw a family close. Those times are harder no matter when Andrew is gone or for how long. You photograph or videotape milestones and share the triumphs on the phone. Phone calls are a blessing when available."

Put yourself in their shoes

I ask you now to sit back and think for a minute. Recall the times your service member has been in a cold, wet "field exercise" or in some hot, dusty, combat mission on the other side of the world being shot at or facing a great possibility of being injured. Or perhaps he or she is somewhere with few comforts and the daily living is pretty miserable. At these times I know your loved one will greatly miss you and wish he or she could relax back in the comforts of home.

I remember being on military training exercises. At times I had to crawl out of my warm sleeping bag in the dark hours of a cold desert night to stand guard with my M-16 rifle loaded with nothing but blanks. I was told and I believed in my heart that service members would fight like they train. With that thought deeply ingrained in my mind, I gladly kept a close eye on my post so that the rest of my unit could sleep safe and sound. If you've never been in the military, it must be hard to understand some of the crazy training we go through, but I'm sure your loved one can share with you some of the fun and not-so-fun stories.

Be sensitive to what your service member may be going through on the other side of the world or in training. Most of the time we will never know all the details or what horror he or she may have seen or what close encounter he or she may have endured.

Can you imagine being a service member? If you were a service member, how would you want your spouse to support you? If you answer that question honestly, you will often be able to let your resentment go.

Nine times out of ten I'm thankful to be the one back home, free to be with my child, cook anything I want to eat, or just sleep in my own cozy bed.

The bottom line is that we (the military couple) chose this way of life. We have to learn how to cope with stressful times. Don't forget to put yourself in your service member's boots every once in a while and give yourself a reality check.

STAGE 4: GETTING INTO THE ROUTINE AS WELL AS TAKING CARE OF YOURSELF

The routine

Now doesn't life seem much better? In approximately week three or four, we are moving right along. In order to stay that way, we should adjust our before and after deployment routines to match our temporary life styles. Routines give you more control over your stress and loneliness because they are constant and unchanging, they keep your mind occupied with the tasks at hand, and they prevent you from going in disorganized directions that again lead to stress.

These adjustments could work with just one loved one, with or without children at home:

★ Getting into nightclothes after doing the dinner dishes

★ Going to bed earlier or later than usual

★ Eating meals earlier or later

★ Going food shopping once or twice a week at a specific time, instead of running out in a tizzy for every item

★ Going through one box of items per week that seems to follow you unpacked from move to move or any other re-organizational or throw-out tasks

★ Being able to do the laundries less frequently or only on a specific day of the week

★ Getting the bills done on a particular evening every week, and so on

Now is the time to create a routine, but part of creating a routine is taking care of yourself. I hate to admit it, but I like being able to wake up at 2:00 A.M., turn on the lamp, and read a little or browse through a catalog of things I usually can't afford to buy. I like doing something enjoyable that I wouldn't do if my other half were there beside me. I know it doesn't sound like much, but if you've been there you'll know what I'm talking about. Little things matter.

Is now a good time to join that gym and plan to go three times a week? Maybe get a new hairstyle? Have you ever asked yourself, "How would I look as a blonde?" This is where the rubber meets the road. Life is all about routine from here on out. Your days will go much smoother if you can establish some sort of regular schedule. The kids will also adjust easier by keeping busy with predictable activities.

Weekdays vs. weekends/Day vs. night: Enjoy meaningful activities

I have noticed that weekdays are easier to deal with, and the nights and weekends seem to be the hardest.

Sara's story

"I'm stressed out during the week, and all I look forward to is the weekend. I then have all this time to sit around and allow my mind to wander to all the thoughts I don't really want to explore. By Sunday evening, I'm usually ready to give my 'bouncing mind' a much-needed break and go back to work. There I can talk with adults and think about something else rather than my situation as a temporarily single parent, lonely, bored, and lovesick."

The time that you and your loved one (days or nights, weekdays or weekends) were together is probably the time you will need to fill with meaningful activities. This could involve volunteer work—if you have time—or you can plan special times with your children. Try something new, something that both you and the children will enjoy.

If you don't have children or time to volunteer, you may have a special hobby you don't spend a lot of time on when your loved one is around. Do what it takes to stay busy with things that make you feel good about yourself. Most important, do something you will enjoy telling your loved one about when you have conversations. Your service member will feel happier that you are doing things that make you happy. It sounds too simple, but try it. You may start to realize the simple things in life are what count.

John once told Rossy, "I'm so glad you keep busy, and you're not just sitting home complaining like so many other wives I hear about." Rossy was overjoyed that John even said that, but it also made her feel good about what she was doing with her time and life while her husband was away.

Michele told me she reads to her child every night, and that she and her child have become very close while their loved one is away. She makes it into a special time for the child. One of my friends summed it up this way: "The more activities you have going on, the quicker time flies. Keep busy!"

Vivian, who has a lot experience with deployments had this to say:

Vivian's story

"Our routine changes both at the departure and at the return. It takes at least two weeks to get everything back on an even keel and about the same when he comes home. The first week seems to be 'Mom's testing week' to see if any of the rules have changed or if Mom is going to be lax about enforcing them. It takes

> at least a week for the kids to remember that just because Dad isn't home does not mean the law has changed. I think when he comes home, he has the most adjustment to make. His patience is not as great as when he is home every day. He is used to doing things on his timetable and has to realize that we have also made our own timetable. So two weeks I think gets everyone back to normal, sometimes less."

Pamper yourself

Remember, part of your new routine is taking care of yourself. Many of us are so busy with kids, jobs, homes, hobbies, and important meetings that we often forget about our own needs. This is especially true during deployments. We often feel so overwhelmed by the extra responsibility that we are the last items on our long list of things to take care of.

In mild cases, we feel burned out and extra grouchy with the kids or lack our normal everyday patience. This burnout phase is common in most spouses and most of us learn to live with it rather than fix it.

Nice ways for you to take care of yourself

1. Join a gym or walking group with other spouses.
2. Pamper yourself once a week, and put it on the calendar.
3. Read a good book.
4. Go to dinner without the kids with another spouse who is home alone.

5. Surround yourself with positive friends.

6. Start eating healthier.

7. Join a bible study or self-help group.

Balance or Burnout

It seems easy to say "balance or burnout," but what a challenge in life to actually find balance. Most of us never take the time to think about balance. We go from one thing to the next and life goes by until one day we wake up and realize something is missing. What is it? Unless we slow down long enough to put some time and deep thought into what it is we are missing, we will never find balance. Until you decide you want balance, it will hang out in front of you all the days of your life. Like most things in life, it's a choice you have to make, and once you make that choice, it will require action on your part. Very few things happen by chance.

Balance during deployments is crucial. We need to get into the mind-set that a deployment is a marathon, not a sprint, and if we are going to make it till the end in good health, we have to find balance.

What is balance? In simple terms balance is having harmony in your mind, body, heart, and soul.

When I think of balance I think of:

Mind/mental: Knowing I'm doing the right thing, constantly learning, improving myself.

Body/physical: Living and eating healthy.

Heart/emotional: Having loving relationships with my
family and friends and seeing the good in others.
Focusing on the positives in life.

Soul/spiritual: Having a deep down, pit-of-the-
stomach knowledge of and relationship with God.
Having a clear conscience that I'm doing my best.

How do you get balance? Write out the words:

Mind
Body
Heart
Soul

One or more of these words are probably jumping out at you right now and you already know which area or areas you may need to add to or take away from. Now . . . go to a place where you can enjoy some quiet, peaceful, uninterrupted time and dwell on these four things. Then think, think, think, what can you do today, this week in one or more of these areas to bring about change? How and where can you add what you're missing?

For me, it was physical fitness. I never seem to have the time or often the motivation to fit it in my day. I know I need to do it, but somehow the days turn into weeks and there I am on the scale wondering why I can't lose weight or why my once hard body is turning into jelly. Since I hate going to the gym or feeling like I don't have the time, I've actually written reminders to do certain exercises on a couple of sticky notes and placed them around the house.

For instance, every time I take a shower, I see a sticky note that says "push-ups and dips." I can do push-ups using the side of the tub and turn around and do tricep dips for the back of my arms. I have a sticky note on the lid of the toilet that says "squats." I'm trying to train myself to do five squats every time I go in the bathroom. The toilet is the perfect height for this exercise. This may sound insane, but I feel if I at least do a few fitness exercises around the house then I won't feel so guilty about not going to the gym. I love to get out and walk, but I know I have to tone the rest of my body as well. I have small weights and a little stool to do arm and shoulder work. This is where I'm starting. All we have to do is start. Start trying to make little changes. Little by little these changes can become habits, and habits can open the door to greater things.

I can only imagine how your mind must be reeling right now thinking of what *you* can do to start.

Why do you need balance? Balance brings about peace and brings your entire life into harmony. You will feel good about yourself. Once you get started you will want to do more and more to fine-tune your life. Once you have balance, you will never want to go back to living a hectic, stressful life. Please don't think I'm living in some la-la land thinking life with balance is stress free. There are always going to be circumstances that require us to be out of balance, but once you start living a life of balance you will never want to be out of balance too long—you will want to live the life you were meant to live.

How do you know when you're out of balance? You feel burned out, frustrated, angry with yourself, angry with life, or exhausted. You feel like you are running in circles, can't do anything to the best of your ability, or never have time to do what you want or enjoy. As much as we all want to stay busy, you have to know the consequences of saying yes to everything and becoming so busy you don't enjoy anything. When everything becomes a chore, and you don't find enjoyment from your everyday activities, you are out of balance.

John Maxwell (#1 leadership expert) says it perfectly: "Learn to say 'no' to the good so you can say 'yes' to the best."

How do you keep balance once you've found it? If only we had a warning alarm every time we ventured off balance! Discover what got you out of balance in the first place and learn to say "No." Many of us get roped into doing things we really don't want to do. We spend countless hours trying to please others and forget to take care of our own families first, the people most important to us. We find ourselves busy with life when all we need to do is slow down and make what we do count. Do it with excellence, passion, heart, etc. I'm not saying become selfish, but enjoy what you do and when you do say "yes," make sure it fits into your priorities. Every one of us has only twenty-four hours in each day. Most of us need eight hours of sleep each night. Most of us will spend approximately three to four hours a day eating, snacking, and cooking. This leaves us with twelve little hours a day. How can you best use your twelve hours? Time waits for no one. No matter what you do, the time you spend will never return.

Learn to laugh more. Humor is good for the soul. If most of your friends including yourself are caught up in the seriousness of military life or life in general, find someone who is funny and makes you laugh and spend time with that person as often as you can. Find a way to add humor in your conversation, laugh at yourself, and don't be afraid of sharing your own humbling, funny experiences. Someone needs to laugh today and you may be the very person who brings that individual that ounce of humor that helps him or her through a tough time.

STAGE 5: LIVING ON LOVE

Quiet moments

When your loved one is away, it is too easy to sit around and dwell on your love, your relationship (both the good and not so good), and your life in general and what it is all about. You may be surprised at the details your mind creates. For example, your mind may want to plan out the rest of your life. I usually try to stop myself before the long-term planning gets out of hand. We can have life plan A, even plan B, but we always follow plan C (which we have usually never planned anyway). It took a few years and many, many broken plans for me to figure this out finally. Now when my husband and I catch ourselves trying to plan out our life's details, we simply tell each other, "You know it will end up being plan C, so why even worry about it?"

Some subjects make the heart grow fonder

With deployment separation, we must discuss matters that most people don't bother with until it's too late. We have to deal with the "power of attorney" issue, which is standard for military couples. We talk about wills and, of course, the "Big D"—in the event of death we need to know the wishes of our loved ones. These issues can be a wake-up call. They really make you think of how some of the small stuff you and your loved one argue about is even smaller than you already know.

Jean's advice

"I guess after sixteen years, it is just part of the package of having a spouse in the military. Any responsible parent or couple should discuss life insurance and wills and the things you need to assure your children's and spouse's emotional and financial security." Each person and couple has their own way of dealing with this topic, but I've found it to be a very loving topic in the end. I encourage all couples to have the "death" conversation. Please refer to chapter 11.

I remember when my husband went to Desert Storm. Wild thoughts were going through my mind—would I ever see him again? I then realized we had never discussed what kind of funeral he would want. Where would he want to be buried? Would he prefer to be buried in his dress greens or dress blues, ribbons or medals? Would he choose Arlington or a local cemetery? I knew if it ever came to the Big D (Death), I would not be in any frame of mind to make those important decisions. Talking about death and all the things that go with it made my husband and I realize how precious our time together is, and that we really are only here for a short while. Talking about these serious issues made us feel close in a new way.

What are the important issues in this life? Is it getting that new kitchen table I've wanted for so long? Or is it just to enjoy what we have and learn to appreciate the little things that will have a lasting meaning? It is the walk in the park hand in hand, discussing our child's future and our future together. It is trying to live a life of peace and harmony, not only with each other, but with our neighbors and families. We spend so much time on the surface that when the feelings get deep, we often panic and begin to sink.

To appreciate

With all the extra responsibilities I have when my husband is away, I have also discovered that I take for granted many of the things he does when he is around. It never seemed necessary to tell him how much I appreciated the little things he does. I don't think I would have ever noticed these things if he didn't go away sometimes. All the neat little things such as taking our son to watch a local ball game while I'm doing something at home or just pitching the ball in the yard with our son on a Saturday afternoon. He is a much better ball-playing role model for our son than I could hope to be. I realize I miss the adult conversation while I'm preparing dinner or folding the clothes.

Many experienced friends share how they show their appreciation and its value during the deployment:

- ★ "I forget about anything he ever did to annoy me because I miss him so much. Time heals all wounds they say, so if he had upset me I don't remember it."

- ★ "I try to stay positive, so I daydream of the things we will do when he returns, the places we will go, the activities we will get the children involved in. I think of all the little everyday chores he gets to take back when he gets home."

- ★ "My husband has repeatedly told me how much he appreciates my support of him and his career in the military and how he appreciates that I've learned to handle everything when he is not available. He tells me he doesn't think he would be in the military if he didn't know that I was there for him when he came home."

- ★ "My husband tells me how much he appreciates me and does special things for me when he is home. Unexpected little things mean a lot. But mostly just saying the words of appreciation mean more."

Remember to tell your service members how much you miss all the little things they do when they are home. When you let your service members know how much they are appreciated, it can be a huge morale booster for our sometimes weary warriors. Let them know you will be the "rock," and they won't worry about anything except getting back home into your arms!

Ways to let your service member know you appreciate him or her

1. Never assume they know. Tell them over and over how proud you are of them.

2. Let them know you miss their personal involvement with the kids.

3. Let them know you miss "just talking" with them.

4. Let them know you respect their honor and loyalty to our country.

5. Reassure them that you will be strong and maintain the home front.

6. Acknowledge little "honey do's" they did for you before deployment.

7. Discuss future family outings that the entire family will enjoy.

The honeymoon just goes on and on

This has to be the best part of being in a military marriage. Your civilian friends will never know what it feels like to have the many, many honeymoons you and I get to enjoy! We are separated from our loved ones for however long, and when we are finally back together, the reunion can be just like the honeymoon all over again. Sometimes it's even better!

Patricia pointed out another benefit that frequent separations have on her marriage: We don't have as much time to get on each other's nerves, and I think we appreciate each other more because our time together is a little more limited than (that of) our friends. In addition, we have only each other to count on because we have no family close enough to count on. I think we appreciate our church family more because they have taken the place of our blood family.

When talking about honeymoons, Tammy told me, "It is the only great part of being separated. Without them to look forward to, I don't think I could bear to do it." I find it just gets better and better with time, like a fine wine. Since we are only human, we all fall into some routine when we are constantly around each other. Just ask your civilian friends. When we endure these forced separations due to deployments, the pleasant surprise is that we get a renewal of passion out of each new honeymoon. Need I say more? You may even catch yourself thinking, "It was all worth it."

It can be difficult during the separation to be around couples who have not been in a long-distance relationship. Lashawn complains, "They do not realize what I am going through when they are loving and kissing each other around me. I don't begrudge them their love, but it's hard for me to see them being affectionate when my love is so far away." Seeing other couples being affectionate while my loved one is away makes me miss him even more and sometimes makes me sad.

★ ★ ★

Tips to Remember

1. Know that the honeymoon will be great. Plan for it!

2. Do not unknowingly play games before a deployment.

3. Prevent your mind from playing "what if" because it can drive you crazy and into a state of depression.

4. Make a decision between you and your loved one that you will commit your relationship to grow in a positive direction.

5. Choose to maintain friendships with good, well-balanced, and positive friends.

6. Make sure both spouses show and verbalize appreciation for what the other is doing or accomplishing—and do it.

7. Be mindful that you are not the only one going through stressful times; we are in this together.

8. Establish a new routine quickly.

9. Substitute the time that was spent with your loved one with meaningful activities.

10. Do not be afraid or ashamed to seek professional help.

Chapter 2

COMMUNICATION

EACH KNOWING WHERE THE OTHER IS COMING FROM

ONE OF THE MOST important lessons I've learned about communications (once again, the hard way) is that you need to understand where your partner is coming from, and your partner needs to know where you are coming from. I cannot stress this enough. Time and time again I thought my husband knew why I felt the way I did or why I asked him to do something a certain way. I would find out later that he didn't have a clue about my reasons (nor did I about his). I thought after several years of marriage that my husband should know where I'm coming from. Our communication is a lot better now than it was in our early years, but I'm still amazed at how we can misunderstand each other. It may sound childish, but if you take the necessary time to explain your thoughts about a situation you feel strongly about, you may avoid a weeklong game-playing session or painful argument.

How to make yourself understood

A short time ago I was feeling a lot of stress at work. I would come home and not really talk about it. Who wants to hear about the stress of work all the time? As much as I tried to act normal and not bring my work home, the stress came out anyway. I was becoming very commanding in my conversations and rushing through everything I did. Of course, I didn't realize any of this or that my husband was feeling brushed off and bossed around. It took a while to understand why this was happening and even longer to overcome this lack of communication.

After an unplanned conversation one morning, it all became apparent that the stress I was feeling at work was in fact following me home. I'm thankful my husband can be so understanding at times. We also realized that he had responded to my behavior with a negative attitude—the whole thing was snowballing! For nothing! A communication breakdown sounds easy enough to figure out, but it gets us every time. Unfortunately, it usually takes about a week of tension before one of us asks, "Is something bothering you?"

It seems strange, but you can misunderstand a whole conversation by the tone of voice—the words are right, but the wrong message comes across. My husband has told me many times that "my tone" can be misleading. I may not even realize I am saying something in any particular tone. I finally told my husband to stop me when I said things in the wrong tone and ask me about them. After a few such conversations, I realized he was right. It's so hard to admit when you're wrong.

If we ever want to become effective communicators we must first learn to listen, listen, and listen. Don't butt in. Don't change the subject quickly. Listen to what the other person just said and reflect back on it. So many of us listen while at the same time we are thinking of what we want to say and when we can butt in to say it. You will be amazed at how difficult it is to stop, listen, and only listen. This lesson is one of the first things I learned in my training as a hostage negotiator: when you listen, really listen, only then can you find out a person's needs.

PHONE TAG

When your loved one is away, you are bound to miss some phone calls from him or her. One friend told me her husband seemed a little mad if she missed his phone call, but he would never say so. Have you noticed or have you ever felt the tension on the other end of the line when you finally talked to your partner after missing a few calls? Have you ever heard your loved one say, "Where were you? Why didn't you answer? You're never home. Didn't you know I'd be calling?" Suddenly, you're on the defensive because you have a long list of reasons why you may haved missed a phone call.

We need to realize that these types of complaints are just our frustrations coming out over not being able to talk with our loved ones. We also need to remember that service members will often stand in long lines just to use the phone for a few minutes, and when they can't get through it's a huge letdown. They are feeling homesick and looking forward to hearing our voice. Think before you react to your loved one's messages. Carrying a cell phone 24/7 during your service member's deployment will help you not miss a call, and it will give the service member comfort to know he or she can reach you anytime. However, we all have to take showers or be places where we may miss a phone call.

When my husband was first stationed in Korea, I would get upset when I couldn't reach him. I'd lie in bed and think, "Where is he? What's he doing? It must be nice to be able to go out and party while I'm here taking care of our child and home!" I would toss and turn all night, and by the next day I was mad. When we would talk, I would blurt out what I was thinking the night before. I could feel the tension on his end—I wanted to hang up. At the same time, though, I knew that if I were the one in Korea, I wouldn't stay in my room! Of course, I would go out and do something, so why didn't I feel he should do the same? I just wanted to tell him I missed him and was thinking of him, but by the time we talked, I was too mad.

Sometimes when you finally get a call through, one or both of you isn't in the talking mood. You begin to think, "Something's going on! What could it be? Did I say something wrong?" The bottom line is, sometimes you or your loved one don't have much to say. Don't take it personally. Just ask whether your mate really wants to talk right now.

E-MAIL/WEBCAM/VOICE OVER INTERNET PROTOCOL (VoIP)/SKYPE . . .

What in the world would we do without e-mail? I honestly feel it's my lifeline during deployment. When I don't hear from my service member via e-mail, I can feel myself starting to get panicky, depressed. Those fearful "what-if" thoughts start to bombard my mind at an increased rate. Even though I've been through this many many times, and I know better, those thoughts still come. I have learned not to allow them to play out. Allowing the depressing "what-if" thoughts to play out makes it hard to get back to your happy thoughts. I feel that is one of the main reasons so many of us get depressed, down, and feeling blah so often during deployments. I hope you will learn, even though the thoughts will come, *not* to allow untrue "what-if" thoughts to play out in your mind. As soon as one pops in your mind, replace it immediately with a positive thought of your service member.

When I was giving a speech at Ft. Bragg, North Carolina, a service member told the audience that during his last deployment he was relocated to an area where he didn't have e-mail or any communications with his spouse for four months! You could have heard a pin drop. I know we were all thinking, "Oh my gosh, I would go crazy." That's reality and it happens. It doesn't mean we have to like it, but it can and sometimes will happen. Hopefully, not for four months, but be aware that communications do go down and it may take a while to get them up and running again.

Once you get on the e-mail, keep in mind that most e-mails

and other electronic communications are closely monitored. Please remember this and do not discuss anything that could be considered OPSEC (Operational Security). It's best to get in the mind-set that whatever you write in e-mail, not only during deployments but anytime, could wind up on the front cover of the morning newspaper or on facebook.

Nowadays, we have an entire assortment of high-tech ways to communicate quickly, easily, and from our own home or cell phones. Webcams are another tool that are available and could be very beneficial for all, especially the kids, who can see Mom or Dad while they're talking to each other in real time. Some VoIP services like Skype are easy to use and best of all are *free*. Not all military units will allow VoIP or have the capabilities. If a webcam is in your future, again, be very careful what you say or do over the airwaves. Think before you act or pose!

Jessica's advice on e-mailing

We are all going to have bad days, sad days, frustrating days and sometimes . . . very angry days.

Jessica says on the days she is very angry, she types out her e-mail so she can vent. She says she types away and gets it all off her chest. *But*, she warns, she never hits the send button after typing one of these e-mails. She advises to wait at least twelve to twenty-four hours, then reread what you've typed, and make the necessary changes as you determine parts of the e-mail that may be too harsh or accusing. Jessica states that after rereading e-mails she has written while angry, she retypes them to get her point across but in a different tone!

Jessica's advice is definitely worth considering. If we would all slow down enough to think before we act, it could help keep the flow of communications on a loving, understanding level. Consider how the service member might feel after receiving an angry, out-of-control e-mail from his or her spouse when the service member has no control over the situation and cannot help. Now, not only is the spouse angry and frustrated, so is the service member. This type of e-mail during deployments is not going to help or solve anything.

You have no way of knowing what type of stress your service member may be under at the time he or she reads an e-mail containing angry, hateful, or other unkind words, and this can cause him or her to become depressed, anxious, unable to sleep, etc. In fact, these e-mails take your service member's focus off the mission, causing him or her and the others in the unit to be at an increased risk of harm.

Is it fair, you ask? Life is not fair, and during deployments, it's often the spouse at home who will have to accept the extra responsibilities and deal with the "angry" times and work through them. This is one reason why having a "battle buddy" is so important. Battle buddies allow us an avenue to vent our anger so we don't have to share it with our service member. Always remember . . . deployments are temporary, and there will be a time when we can share the situation or angry thoughts we had.

A "battle buddy" is that trusted someone who knows what you are going through and who most likely is going through it too. You will each need to call on each other at different times during the deployment for "sanity checks," "anger at hubby checks," "kids driving you crazy checks," "blah-day checks," and of course "shopping therapy checks." Everyone needs a battle buddy or two during deployments.

WHOSE LIFE IS MORE MISERABLE?

Now you're both on the phone or on the computer ready to talk, trying to share your feelings and letting each other know what's happening in your lives. All of a sudden you're in a "Whose life is more miserable?" contest. Guess what? There are no winners in this game. Stop it before it starts! First, you can't compare apples and oranges, home life to deployment, changing diapers to a business trip, or temporary duty in a foreign country to staying home and taking care of the kids. Second, it will only make you both feel worse. Sure, you want to let your loved one know you're unhappy without him or her, but dwelling on the loneliness, stress, and general craziness you are both enduring is not going to help or change the situation.

Most of the difficult times can be discussed when you're back together, when you can reassure your service member you're not blaming him or her for what you're going through. Jackie writes, "Why worry him, he has enough worries of his own. If you burden him with all the little ups and downs, then it makes for a very long deployment." Even if your mate's life is not as miserable as yours, be happy for him or her. If the tables were turned, you would want your spouse to be happy for you. We all know misery loves company, but wait till your company can actually be in your arms.

DO NOT READ BETWEEN THE LINES

I have to add this because most of my friends have admitted to reading between the lines. Kay said, "I think everyone tries to find the information that we know they are hiding from us. I feel that he is trying to spare me from his upset and will avoid certain conversations."

For example, my friend Gale was talking with her husband when he was on deployment in Bosnia for six months. They were on the phone and he wasn't saying much, but she didn't bother to ask why. For a whole week it bothered her. The next time they talked, she discovered his commander had been in the room on the day of their last conversation. Not only was her husband uncomfortable talking at that time, but he could not even tell his wife that his commander was nearby because of security concerns.

Don't try to read between the lines, there may not be anything there. Ask questions if you hear a tone of voice you're not sure of. It never hurts to ask. Knowing your service member is going on a mission will not change that fact and will only make you worry.

WHO HANGS UP FIRST?

Now it's time to say good-bye and hang up the phone. Sounds easy, but I know from personal experience it isn't. Many I've talked with have the same problem. It goes something like this:

"I love you."
"I love you too, I'll talk with you next time, okay? I love you."
"I love you too."
"Well, I guess we'd better hang up."
"Yeah, you know I love you."
"I love you too. Call me next week."
"I will. I love you."
"I love you too."

Conversations like this can go on and on. The problem is, neither of you wants to be the first to hang up. What is a loving spouse to do? The longer you are away from each other, the longer it can take to hang up. The phone bill can really suffer at this point. One trick is say, "Okay, let's count to three and hang up. One, two, three, CLICK." Just do it or you will never get off the phone!

Janet once confided, "On some days it is really hard to hang up. Even when you don't have anything you really need to say, that link is still there, and it is hard to say good-bye. I personally don't like to be the one to say good-bye first. I like to hold on to the link as long as possible."

COMMUNICATIONS WITH YOUR PARENTS, FRIENDS, OR IN/OUT-LAWS!

Have you noticed during deployment you definitely call home or talk to friends more? What about the in-laws or, as some of you call them, the out-laws? I know for me, on a Friday night—when I would normally be looking forward to a nice dinner with my husband before the start of the weekend—when he's deployed, I burn up the phone line. First, I have the time and, second, it gets me through a time when I would have been with him. I love talking to my mom, sister, friend, or anyone who has time for me! I feel very fortunate to have people in my life whom I enjoy talking to who love me and understand me. I'm not sure what I would do without good conversation. I love to talk!

During deployments I feel many of us try not to become a burden on our family and friends and we may conceal our fears and emotions to a point we almost live a facade! I have found that even though I love talking with my family and friends, I don't feel like (if they're not military) they understand what I'm going through, so why bother them with my loneliness, fears, whining, etc. Or, if I'm talking to my military friends, most of them are going through their own issues, so we end up keeping it all in. I have found I don't want to transfer my fear or worries to my family. They are already worried enough. Especially the service member's family. Having my own child, I can imagine how difficult it must be for those whose child is in harm's way. It's hard enough having your other half "over there." I admire the men and women who have endured having both their spouse and their child serving our country!

I have found it very sad when I hear spouses talk about how their in-laws drive them crazy during deployments. I've heard spouses complain when the in-law calls and wants information. How else are the parents supposed to get information about their child? I know not all in-laws are nice, and they may deserve to be called "out-laws," but they deserve some information. One solution may be for you to call your in-laws once a week and give them an update. That way, you make it part of your routine, when you know you will have the time and don't have to feel guilty rushing off the phone because you are trying to get the kids to soccer practice or dinner on the table. Another solution may be to add them to the e-mail distro list for the unit newsletter. Many units are using virtual family readiness websites that parents may be allowed to use as well. This will help them feel like they are part of the unit and provide direct information on how their loved one in theater is doing.

Try to remember, this is their child "over there" and, understandably, they have fears and worries and you are most likely their only line of communication. If they didn't love their child, they wouldn't be calling. I hope you can try to be understanding. One day your child may be "over there" and you may be the one calling. I'm a firm believer that how we treat others comes back to us.

PERSONAL SECURITY TO THE PUBLIC

If you've been around the military for any time at all, you've probably heard the terms OPSEC (Operational Security), COMSEC (Communication Security), and perhaps other "SECs." Most spouses don't pay much attention to the military jargon that doesn't pertain to family life. It seems to go in one ear and out the other. I'm writing this section for you and your families own personal security. I think of it as PERSEC (personal security, not a real military acronym).

I can't tell you how many times I've been at the local grocery store and overheard spouses discussing their service members' deployment and other sensitive information that anyone could hear. If you're a military spouse and your service member is away from home, you need to realize that information shouldn't be public knowledge. None of us does this intentionally, but personal information can slip out that may put yourself and our families in danger.

During my law enforcement career, I remember many deputies discussing how wives should not display on their homes, vehicles, or T-shirts that their service members are deployed. Women who do so may become bigger targets of crime than before. For example, in a housing community, many military families will place yellow ribbons, signs, banners, and flags on their homes and vehicles when the service member is on deployment. I know we all want to show our support, but to the local criminal, you may as well be displaying an Easy Target sign that says "I am home alone." Local criminals will know who is military and who is not in your community. There are more eyes on you than you know. Please continue to show your support for the troops, but place the yellow ribbons in community areas instead of on your mailbox or on your front porch and in your yard. An exception to this rule would be if all the homes in your area display yellow ribbons or American flags, in which case, by all means, display away! Try to fit in with the norm of your neighborhood.

One common mistake for PERSEC is letting too many people know you are home alone. Some spouses seek sympathy from others by letting them know their loved ones are away, but this may backfire. For example, you could be at your corner gas station/quick stop, where you know the store clerk. He or she may ask you out of genuine concern, "Has your service member been deployed with all the other service members?" You should never respond with, "Yes, and he or she will be gone for a whole year!" Little do you know who is standing in one of the store aisles overhearing you. The criminal can then identify your car and find out where you live in the local area. That person may even act concerned and gather more information from the unsuspecting store clerk or even follow you home, knowing you are home alone. I don't want to scare you, but there have been more reports of burglary and rape than you care to know about. Local criminals who knew the victim was home alone conducted most of these crimes. Just being a woman makes you a target, but a military spouse whose service member is on deployment has extra risks.

Who needs to know you're "home alone"?

My friend Deb warned me about a potential personal security risk that occurred at her duty station. One of the local cable companies was offering half off the cable bill for spouses of deployed service members. First, I feel this is very generous of the cable company, and I'm sure all the right motives were involved when the company offered this nice deal. But then the questions came up: Who would have access to the sensitive information that spouses who signed up for this special offer were home alone? How many employees of the cable company could gain access to this list? We all know, in the wrong hands this information could then be used in an unlawful manner. In simpler times, we never used to worry about this type of danger, but that was then and this is now. Be careful in accepting special offers that allow anyone to access your home address along with the knowledge you are home alone or any other "sensitive information."

If you've ever been a victim of a home break-in, you may have learned the following information a little too late. I hope by sharing what I've learned as a victim of a home break-in, along with the extensive experience during my law enforcement years, that you will take heed and never become a crime statistic.

Before you move into any neighborhood, ask around and find out if there have been any reports of break-ins. You can simply walk around and ask some of the neighbors. If you see bars on the windows of several houses, that is a sure sign. If the neighborhood is not new, and you see several "home security" signs placed in the front yards, they may indicate a break-in problem. Pay attention to local news to find out about crimes in the neighborhood where you live.

I want to explain the mode of operation that most local criminals will often use to conduct break-ins:

First, they usually scout out the area and look for the easiest target (see Tip #1 in the proceeding list). Once the criminal has spotted an easy target, the next step is to approach the house. In most cases, the criminal does not want a confrontation. He or she would prefer no one to be home so that as many valuables as possible can be taken as quickly as possible. Many will approach the home and knock or ring the doorbell. The criminal is checking to see if anyone is home and/or if any dogs are in the residence. This is why it's very important for you or your kids to always speak through—not open—the door, letting whoever is there know someone is home. I know many of us leave our children at home and tell them not to answer the door, but this may lead to a break-in. You can tell them to say through the door that their parent cannot come to the door at this time. Reiterate to *never* open the door.

If no one answers after several knocks, the criminal will begin the break-in, perhaps signaling some buddies to join him or her and then go to the back door or backyard to gain entry. Law enforcement people have told me some criminals will carry a bag of hot dogs to feed any dogs they encounter during a theft.

Once the criminal or criminals gain entry into your home, they usually start in the master bedroom. Often the first items stolen will be jewelry boxes, lockboxes, and any guns, weapons, or cash. They usually intensely search the master bedroom for these items. Next, they will look for electronics or expensive souvenirs you may have collected over the years. Then, it will be anything of value that the criminal can sell or keep for personal use.

If you have a firebox to keep all your important papers in, don't lock it, or lock it and leave the key in it! Should you ever become a victim of a break-in, most criminals will only rummage through the box looking for guns, cash, or other valuables. Most are not interested in your important papers, and they will leave them behind. If the box is locked, the intruders will take the whole box, thinking there must be cash, guns, and so on, inside. They will more than likely dump your important papers in a trash bin later. The box can still be fireproof if unlocked.

In the event that you ever arrive home and notice your front or back door has been kicked in or any entry has been gained into your residence, leave immediately, go to a neighbor's, or drive down the street and call law enforcement. Keep an eye on your residence in case you observe the criminals leaving. Do not go back into your home until it has been cleared by the police.

Four major tips on preventing a break-in:

Tip #1: Prevent your home from being an easy target

★ Have a professional security alarm installed, if possible.

★ Cut any tall or overgrown bushes from around the house because they offer great concealment during and after a break-in.

★ Consider owning large dogs as a deterrent, especially if you keep them inside the house.

★ Be alert if you suspect break-ins are occurring in your neighborhood, and never leave windows open while you are away for any length of time.

★ Do not leave keys under the mat or under flowerpots close by the door. Find a better place to hide your emergency house key.

★ Place good dead bolts on all your doors because doors without dead bolts are very easy to kick in.

★ Keep your house and doorways well lit. Motion sensors on the corners of the house will work well for the area around the house. Some criminals have been known to unscrew lights near the doorway, so make sure you buy fixtures that hinder or prevent easy access.

★ Stop deliveries of newspapers or mail that might pile up on the driveway or overflow your mailbox. This is a sure sign the occupants are out of town. If possible, ask a trusted neighbor to collect the papers and mail, and offer to reciprocate.

★ Set your lights on timers when you go away so that they

turn on during the hours you are usually home. Put a radio or TV on a timer so that it appears you are home. Keep your house looking lived in as much as possible, especially during the Christmas holidays when so many of us go out of town.

★ Be aware of break-ins in your area when you are planning a trip out of town, and load your vehicle as discreetly as possible. If you have a garage, pull the vehicle in and load it with the garage door closed.

Tip #2: Beware of strangers

★ If a stranger knocks on your door while you or your children are home, never, never open the door. Always speak through the door without opening it, letting the stranger know someone is home. Speak loudly, and tell the stranger, "We don't take solicitors." Make sure it is clear that someone is in the house.

★ Get into the habit of locking all doors leading into your home when you are home alone, especially during the hours of 9 A.M. to 5 P.M. Most people work during those hours and the kids are in school then, so the majority of break-ins occur during that time frame. Of course, plenty occur in the hours of darkness too.

Tip #3: Notice your neighborhood

★ Be aware of your surroundings at all times. If you see a suspicious vehicle or person in your neighborhood, call the police.

★ Be familiar with the vehicles your neighbors drive so that you will know if you see one that doesn't belong.

Tip #4: Protect your valuables

★ Do not keep all your valuables in the master bedroom, especially if you travel and you don't have a security system.

Safety tip

If your service member drives the same vehicle to work every day, and all of a sudden that vehicle never moves from your driveway, you may as well hang the sign out, HOME ALONE. Move each vehicle that is normally driven and drive your service member's vehicle while he or she is away. Keep things looking normal around your home.

I will leave the OPSEC and COMSEC up to the military officials to keep their families informed. For your PERSEC, think before you discuss being home alone with anyone other than your close friends and family. Even then, don't discuss details over cordless phones or cell phones. Keep the yellow ribbons in the house and not on the outside. Don't give signals that could target you as a military spouse who's home alone.

★ ★ ★

TIPS TO REMEMBER

1. Try to grasp what your partner's thinking and reasoning is in your conversations.
2. Practice listening so that when you listen, you're really listening. Only then can you find out a person's needs and wants.

3. Do not read between the lines.

4. Be aware that the service member will often wait in long lines to use the phone.

5. Avoid comparing home front life to combat or training missions.

6. Do not let everyone know you are home alone and cause your loved one undo worry. He or she has enough to contend with during the deployment.

7. Take the precautions listed to ensure your home is not an easy target for break-ins.

8. Be aware of your surroundings and neighborhood at all times.

9. Be careful when agreeing to sign up for special offers that enable unknown people to acquire your home address and the knowledge that you are living alone.

Chapter 3

FINANCIAL HARDSHIP: A LONG-DISTANCE BUDGET

BEFORE ANY DEPLOYMENT you absolutely must discuss finances. What one spouse thinks is okay to spend money on, the other is thinking "no way." As you know, there will be some extra money coming in during deployment. How you spend it can make or break a relationship. Finances is one topic you both need to agree on. You need to set financial goals, guidelines, and priorities before the deployment. We've all heard the horror stories about how waste, neglect, and credit crises can cripple a family and a relationship.

THE URGE TO SPLURGE

What better way to make me feel better when my husband is away than to spend money! I hate to say it, but spending money makes me feel better. I tell myself, "Some people drink, some people smoke, and some go out to bars. I just like to go to Wal-Mart and buy little things." It never fails—when I go to these places, I always find something I need or have been wanting. I get to the checkout line and fifty dollars is gone, just like that. I ask myself, "Why did I even come here?" A treat doesn't have to cost much. It could be something I'd been wanting for the kitchen, a new rug, bath bubbles, or anything. I tell myself "I deserve it."

To my regret, my splurging and trying to maintain two households when my husband was in Korea got us into a $5,000 credit card debt just after we took a $10,000 consolidation loan to pay off our other credit debt. It seemed impossible to get out of debt. Some of my friends have $15,000 or even $30,000 in credit card debt. The more my husband was deployed, the more I wanted to spend or the more unexpected expenses seemed to pop up. I would buy things we needed—things for the house, for our son, for our dog, bird, and fish, you name it. I would always justify my spending by saying "we need it."

Kim's spending

"I'm guilty; yes, I spend more money when Andrew is away. I think that happens mostly because we try to stay busy, and doing other things helps keep your mind occupied so that the loneliness doesn't hit as hard."

Lee-ray's warnings

"I don't have anyone to remind me that we need to save. As long as I send my husband his money, I can spend guilt free. I know it's wrong, but I do it anyway."

Many others have told me similar stories, and the bottom line is you have to become disciplined. Get rid of the credit cards, and find a way to stop careless spending before it cripples your family for years to come. When I calculated our debt and figured out how long it would take us to pay it off, I nearly had a heart attack. Eventually, after some sacrifices, we finally got out of debt. I still have the urge to splurge, but if my debit card won't cover a purchase, I don't buy it.

Credit card advice

★ Find the lowest fixed rate interest credit card.

★ Have only one credit card for emergencies.

★ Make it a priority to pay off all charges.

★ Keep the card out of your wallet.

THE WICKED PHONE BILL

Just when you've been charging recklessly and you know you've overspent your monthly budget, the phone rings. It's not a creditor—it's your loved one calling from a faraway country, and every minute you talk is costing more than you can afford. This expense tends to put pressure on you to cut the whole conversation short. Just try to tell your spouse everything you want to in as little time as possible.

The problem is, this is the time that butting in becomes commonplace, because you don't want to leave anything out. There can also be the added stress of trying to read between the lines and figure out if there is any hidden message in the conversation. In places like Korea, a yearlong tour can cost a family dearly. The long-distance phone bill is one expense that many of us forget to include in the household budget. Many people, including me, call their families more during a deployment.

Frances's phone calls

Frances told me that when her husband is away she makes more domestic calls to her family for sympathy. She is also quick to remind us that "in today's military, more opportunities exist for the service member to call home for free. Look into what you are entitled to get." Some long-distance companies are finally catching on to the hardship of a long-distance lifestyle and are offering reasonable rates. It pays to shop and compare.

Even with free calls offered in many combat zones, service members don't want to stand in the long lines and/or have to depend on the phone lines working at all. It's being reported that many are buying phones with international capabilities and making calls to the family whenever they want. This is a huge problem that needs to be addressed. First, it costs the service member tons of money for this service and second, and most important, it can become a major Operational Security (OPSEC) violation.

There are times when and reasons why the phone system may not work. One could be an important "high-target" mission that needs to be kept "top secret." If the service member decides to call home before one of these missions and slips the tongue with *any* tidbit of information the enemy can use, the whole mission and the lives of the service members involved could be at risk. Trust me, the enemy is listening!

Young and inexperienced service members do not see the big picture and do not intentionally violate OPSEC, but it happens too often and needs to stop. For this very reason, many units do not allow the use of private phones, so if your service member is out trying to purchase an international phone beware. The charges are outrageous and it may not be authorized.

What is OPSEC?

Operational Security. Keeping any and all specific operational information guarded. Things like time and place, such as when the unit/ship is landing or taking off. Any type of missions you may think your service member will be involved in. Specific locations of your service member (i.e., Balad, Afghanistan). Never e-mail rosters or lists of spouses with e-mails and/or phone numbers to anyone outside your group. Shred old rosters. Do not use rank or full names of service members. Remember, sensitive information can be used to target you or our military.

STEALING FROM SAVINGS TO PAY CHECKING

If you've ever had to take money out of savings to deposit into checking, so that the checks or e-bills don't bounce, you'll know where I'm coming from. Anyone who is in a long-distance relationship is sure to face unexpected expenses during the deployment or separation. Moving funds from savings to checking on a monthly basis will get you into trouble fast. Wake up and go over your spending with a fine-tooth comb, and find out where you're overspending. Make a budget and put it on paper. If you can't cut back on anything, then you're living outside your income. This situation will have to be corrected.

I hate to play the savings to checking game. Before my husband left for Korea, we did not imagine what a financial drain his extra living expenses would be on our family.

Christy's financial situation

Christy told me anytime she and her husband have to maintain two households, it's a financial burden. Even though he may be staying in the barracks or quarters, he still needs to eat, buy shower stuff, go out, and, basically, have a life.

We have to recognize that when one spouse is away, it's going to cost more. It took a few deployments and close calls with the checkbook before my husband and I realized this. I've learned to cut back on my spending while he is away. Some unexpected expense always seems to crop up and take that extra $100 or so you thought you had saved in your account.

If you must make transfers to cover these expenses, be sure to let your spouse know about it. If any accounts come up short, the military will hold both of you responsible. You'll both suffer the repercussions, no matter who made the withdrawal. The service member may even receive a reprimand from his or her commander if this occurs. I've known service members who the military removed from certain duty positions or units because of a failure to maintain their finances. And it doesn't matter to the military if the spouse at home is blowing the budget or the service member.

Military couples should never take finances lightly. If your service member is away, he or she is counting on you to take care of the bills and keep a balanced checkbook. I've often told my husband this can be a scary responsibility, especially for young couples. Your family and the future of your family depend on you to make smart financial decisions.

Many military families have separate accounts and checkbooks. They use one account to pay most of the bills, and the other may be a local account used for fun or vacation savings. If a service member is going on a long deployment, he or she may need an additional account set up with a predetermined amount deposited into it each payday. That way, you don't have to worry about keeping track of who is spending what.

BEWARE OF UNEXPECTED EXPENSES

Pre-deployment expenses

Even after twenty-three-plus years of active-duty service, my husband still spends money on deployments. You would think that with foot lockers, wall lockers, attic space, under-the-bed space, a spare bedroom, closets, and every other nook and cranny in our home overflowing with military garb—enough to open a fully equipped surplus store and then some—he would have what he needs to deploy. He has green stuff, tan stuff, black stuff, bags, pouches, straps, holsters, and on and on and on. But oh no, each and every deployment—and there have been more than I can count on my hands and toes—he needs more stuff! What is a spouse to do?

Technology is continually changing and so is "military gear" and electronics. If your service member wants a new electronic gadget that will help him or her take the edge off being away from home and provide entertainment, by all means, try to come up with the funds and buy it. I'm not saying go into serious debt. Now may be a good time to ask family members to pitch in and provide an early Christmas or birthday gift. Maybe we could learn to "save" and plan for some of these items if we don't wait until the last minute.

Don't even think about suggesting a flea market or surplus store, like I did. The garb our service members are seeking to take to combat is the latest, greatest, hot-off-the-production-line type of staff. It often takes our wonderful military time and lots of moola to catch up with many of these products. Our service members usually don't have time to wait and, after all, they deserve the best.

Some common items you may want to start a deployment fund for are Under Armour and other high-end clothing, specialty socks, extra ammo pouches, extra holsters (ask no questions, and you will get no lies!), any and all of the latest electronic gadgets, video games, music, books (electronic if possible—have you looked at the new Kindle on Amazon or Nook at Barnes and Noble?), and the list goes on and on.

Can you hear the ka-ching ka-ching of the credit card now? Oh yes, many of your service members will remind you that "combat pay" will cover these items. That may be true, but for now how are you paying for it? If you decide to charge these pre-deployment expenses on credit cards, don't forget to remind your service member later about the bill you are paying off using the "combat pay"!

Now that you've spent an arm and a leg to get your service member ready for deployment, you start thinking about being home alone for an extended period and of some items you may need to get by with. For instance, my husband used to mow our lawn with an old push mower. We decided before one deployment to purchase a nice riding lawn mower (ka-ching ka-ching). I had experienced a back injury, so push mowing was out of the question for me. Some spouses who have small children will most likely have to pay a yard service during deployments (beware of who knows you're home alone). Some couples will look into purchasing newer vehicles. Most service members don't want to risk having their spouse break down on the side of the road during deployments.

Did I mention the pre-deployment vacation you will want to take? Take advantage of all the deals out there for service members and their families. (See "Resources/Support Groups" at the end of the book for great websites.)

Oh yeah, don't forget, you will most likely want some family photos taken too. With the ease of digital cameras nowadays, this doesn't have to cost too much. Do take the time to have them taken.

Deployment expenses

If your budget didn't take a hit with the pre-deployment expenses, get ready—Murphy (as in Murphy 's Law) is alive and well. In fact, Murphy thrives during most deployments. It never fails: things break, burn, crack, leak, blow up, crash, and do anything else Murphy can throw at you during deployments. It's going to happen. When it does, try not to have a meltdown. Take a deep breath, call a friend, get some help, and deal with the situation.

If money is an issue, there are programs in place that can help with emergencies or hardships. Of course, there are the programs within the military that help, but some situations call for outside help. Most of these and other types of assistance are available through your unit's leadership. Never be afraid to let your leadership know you need help. Most of your leaders have been around many years and have knowledge of all sorts of avenues to assist you. But remember, they can never help if they are not aware of a problem to begin with.

Operation Homefront is one organization that has helped thousands of military families.

The following information is given on its website (www. operationhomefront.net):

Operation Homefront Services

Emergency and financial assistance grants, food, wounded warrior housing, vehicle repair/donation, moving assistance, computers, furniture, and holiday programs.

Mission Statement: Operation Homefront provides emergency morale and assistance to our troops, to the families they leave behind and to wounded warriors when they return home.

Who We Serve: E1–E6 and all ranks of wounded officers. Operation Homefront has processed more than 200,000 cases, including more than 8,100 involving wounded warriors. Operation Homefront serves all branches of the armed forces, including active duty, Guard and Reserve.

Here's how they would handle a typical case:

1. Operation Homefront takes a call from a young family who, in addition to the emotional stress of deployment, does not have the experience or financial resources to handle a crisis that normally occurs in military life.
2. They work with local service providers (such as car mechanics or general contractors), media partners and Web site visitors to request specific assistance (such as car transmission repair services) and then coordinate those services with the family, typically within 24–72 hours.
3. After the crisis is over, case managers (often experienced military wives themselves) work with the families to better prepare their household finances, outline the resources available through the military and introduce them to a community of other military families to help them develop a social support network.

4. Few clients need assistance a second time, and many come back to volunteer with other families.

Homefront Online: Operation Homefront also operates *Homefront Online*, the online magazine and Web community for military spouses.

Allison's husband, a service member, was wounded in Iraq, but not serious enough for the military to assist her with funds for her to travel to Germany to be with him. Needless to say, she was extremely upset knowing her husband was injured. Operation Homefront stepped in and provided her round-trip airfare so she could visit him and spend time by his side during his recovery.

More deployment expenses: Care packages and kids' activities

Care packages, those periodic boxes of goodies sent to service members who are on deployment, can also have an effect on your finances. Most of the requests are for favorite goodies that our service members can't buy where they may be located. I know my husband would love to open a care package every week, but money talks when funds are short. At times like these, again, call on family members and friends who want to help out and have them send your loved one some of the things on his or her wish list. Care packages are very important—they let the service member know he or she is always in your thoughts. The new "flat rate" fee the postal service offers has saved military families tons of money, and there is the morale boost our service members get from receiving care packages. "Go postal service."

Who says a care package has to cost a lot anyway? Be creative! Sometimes you can send homemade cards and a homemade CD of your spouse's favorite songs or a video of the kids saying hello. Once, the spouses of all the service members in my husband's unit met together and brought different things to put in a care package for every service member deployed, married or single. It was a lot of fun, and the service members really got a kick out of it. It was also a nice time to get together with the other spouses, and the kids loved it too.

When your service member is on deployment, you will most likely take the kids to more activities than usual to get everyone's mind off the sadness of Dad or Mom being gone. This expense should also be part of the financial plan you make before deployment.

Post-deployment/midtour expenses

Whether it's midtour or post-deployment we all want to go somewhere or celebrate in a big way. Midtour we have only a short time, so we feel we have to make the most of it. If the kids are in school, we may have to postpone the vacation till post-deployment, but you can bet you will be going out to dinner, seeing movies, making purchases, and so on—ka-ching ka-ching.

Post-deployment most of us will plan some sort of vacation away from home. We need to start planning for this way before post-deployment. Also, for all those things that broke that we didn't have the money to buy a new one and we used duct tape, Velcro, or Super Glue to fix, now we'll be able to spend the money for the proper repair since hubby or honey is home.

Gifts

Your service member will most likely bring you gifts from his or her faraway travels. This will need to come out of the budget. Plan for the little or "big" surprises you may be receiving!

If your service member is a female and you have already fixed all the things that broke, beware she may need a "girlie fix." Provide her some quality time at the spa, hair salon, or nail salon. And did I mention "shopping therapy"? That's a must! Some of us girlies, whether service members or spouses, may need or want "beauty enhancement" treatments. The prices of some of these treatments have become more affordable and very enticing. I must say, the older I get the more enticing some of these treatments are looking! After all, we will justify that wrinkles are caused by stress, and if deployment isn't stress I don't know what stress is. Ka-ching ka-ching.

WHY DO YOU NEED A BUDGET, AND PROFESSIONAL GUIDANCE?

If the previous pages aren't enough to make your head spin, the fact that getting into financial trouble is one of the leading causes of stress in a relationship and one of the main factors leading to divorce. This is why it's one of the most important areas in your marriage, yet far too many of us take it much too lightly. We are now paying the consequences and playing catch-up with our retirement funds.

I can't tell you how many stories I hear over and over about how finances ruin what is supposed to be a happy deployment homecoming! If you don't sit down and come up with a budget and plan for your finances before the deployment—or actually right now; don't wait till deployment—trust me, the money will disappear and you will never know how or where it went.

Deployments and receiving combat pay and other specialty pay within the military can offer opportunities like never before to enhance your savings.

One program that you must look into is The Department of Defense Savings Deposit Program (SDP). This is a different program from the Thrift Savings Plan (TSP). "This plan was established to provide members of the uniformed services serving in a designated combat zone the opportunity to build their financial savings." (Due to how quickly changes occur within the military, I'm hesitant to quote the allowable amount accepted and generous interest rate offered with this program.)

Trust me, check it out at www.dfas.mil (Defense Finance and Accounting Service). Type in "Savings Deposit Program" in the "Search" tool bar. There are plans to expand the program's services to offer different options of saving. Don't miss out—start saving now!

Don't be like me and think if you can't save at least $100 per month it's not worth saving. Any amount of saving is better than none. If you must, start out with $25 to $50 per month and watch how the compound interest starts to add up. Once you see it grow, you will find ways to add to it. Starting is the most important part of saving.

Financial professionals

I highly recommend a program that is being offered on several military installations, sponsored by The Dave Ramsey Financial Peace University. The following information is adapted from its website, www.daveramsey.com/military/home.

Financial Peace Military Edition **is an intensive training course in personal finance** that help service members **strategically and effectively remove debt and build wealth.** According to the website, "more than 12,000 military families have already experienced the benefits" of its 13-lesson, video-driven course.

Because Financial Peace Military Edition provides service members with a sound financial plan during their times of activation or deployment, whether TDY or PCS, they need not be preoccupied with concerns about financial stress at home (which otherwise can mount during the tour of duty) and are "free to focus on their unit's mission with peace of mind."

Here's how it works:

A small group gets together to view the course (one lesson per week for 13 weeks) in DVD format, taught by personal finance expert Dave Ramsey. The course "covers everything from budgeting and paying off debt to retirement and charitable giving." A workbook, specifically designed for service members and their families, which addresses questions and provides statistics related to military service, is included.

The average family **pays off $5,300** in consumer debt and puts **$2,700 into savings** during the 13-week program.

I feel the locations and numbers of classes are only going to increase over time as the success of this program expands.

There are many reputable financial investment brokers who provide expert advice and guidance. I've read enough books to know that my husband and I needed professional guidance. We also wanted to sit down face-to-face to go over our financial situation and find an advisor whom we trusted and could build a relationship with.

Financial planning in the military—because of frequent relocations, buying, selling, renting, tax laws changing from state to state, spouses income starting, ending, or changing with new deployments, and so forth—can be confusing, to say the least.

There are several financial organizations that cater to and/or are founded by prior military members who know our service members' needs. Following is a partial list of resources, not listed in any certain order, but a great place to start your financial freedom journey.

First Command Financial Services: www.firstcommand.com
United Services Automobile Association (USAA): www.usaa.com
Military Officers Association of America (MOAA): www.moaa.org
Military Benefit Association (MBA): www.militarybenefit.org
Military OneSource: www.militaryonesource.com
Military Money: www.militarymoney.com; a magazine that offers a vast assortment of financial readiness resources for the military and various other aspects of military life

I'm not suggesting these organizations are any better than others; however, it's refreshing to sit down with our advisor and not have to explain what we are talking about when we use terms like TDY (temporary duty), TSP (Thrift Savings Plan), LES (Leave and Earnings Statement), SDP (Savings Deposit Program), SGLI (Servicemembers' Group Life Insurance), VGLI

(Veterans' Group Life Insurance), PCS (permanent change of station), and all the other military acronyms we find ourselves using in our everyday language.

Why you shouldn't wait: A personal story

Once my husband and I decided to seek professional financial advice we were in for a shock and had to face some unpleasant realities. When our advisor explained to us about "compound interest" and we could see on paper how we had missed out on growing wealth slowly, over time, little by little, and how a little money saved every month would have been growing into a hefty retirement/savings fund, we felt like complete idiots. We wished we had taken advantage of compound interest throughout our entire working life. What were we thinking?

Finally, after our advisor had spent hours with us coming up with a workable plan where we could still enjoy life (in a more frugal way) and save for retirement, we realized we were going to need life insurance after the military. Again, if only we had started earlier, the rates would have been much cheaper and maintainable. We decided on a plan that we felt we could afford, and guess what? You're not going to believe this: we found out we were *both* declined life insurance! Yes, my active duty military service member—serving just fine, no profiles, deploying often, and so on—was denied coverage due to a prior brain tumor (noncancerous). I was denied as well due to a breast MRI that was declined by Tricare, which caused red flags to raise for the underwriters! Still, to this day, my mammograms have come back clean. Only because I was denied an MRI was I told I couldn't be insured. Can you imagine? We honestly feel like healthy adults (not much over forty), and to think, we can't obtain life insurance. I know we have the VGLI (Veterans' Group Life Insurance) to fall back on, but it would be nice to have choices.

The bottom line: don't wait. Get your financial future in order. Things happen and change every day, and one day you may wake up and be uninsurable or find yourself needing emergency funds to cover anything from medical crises to large-ticket items. We need to plan and save for life's uncertainties. With the proper guidance and planning, becoming debt free is obtainable.

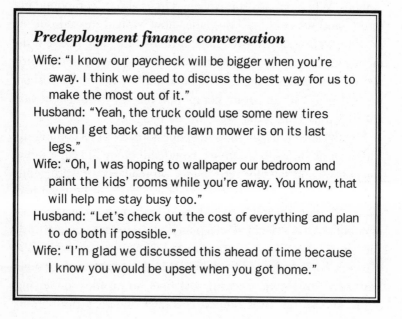

Predeployment finance conversation

Wife: "I know our paycheck will be bigger when you're away. I think we need to discuss the best way for us to make the most out of it."

Husband: "Yeah, the truck could use some new tires when I get back and the lawn mower is on its last legs."

Wife: "Oh, I was hoping to wallpaper our bedroom and paint the kids' rooms while you're away. You know, that will help me stay busy too."

Husband: "Let's check out the cost of everything and plan to do both if possible."

Wife: "I'm glad we discussed this ahead of time because I know you would be upset when you got home."

★ ★ ★

TIPS TO REMEMBER

1. Couples, remind yourselves that you grow with each hardship in ways you don't yet understand.

2. Remember, couples living apart will most often find it a financial burden.

3. Understand that unexpected expenses will alway come up: count on it, save for it, and discuss it prior to deployment, not after.

4. Stop using credit cards. If you absolutely have to charge something, make it a priority to pay it off.

5. Write out a budget and plan for pre-deployment, deployment, and past-deployment spending.

6. Seek and obtain financial wisdom and planning.

7. Strive to become debt free.

Chapter 4

INFIDELITY

EVERY LONG-DISTANCE RELATIONSHIP is tested by at least the temptation of infidelity by the loved one who is away or the loved one at home. I'd like to start this chapter with a few words about the mind games we play when we suspect our spouse of being disloyal.

If you are already having fears about infidelity before the deployment, do not kid yourself into believing they will go away with your dearest. They will only multiply with his or her departure. They will come to consume your thoughts, cause you to look for anything out of the ordinary in your loved one's voice, e-mail, letters, or actions. You will turn the slightest thing into a "sign" that something is going on. Suspicions will drive you crazy. Make the time before the departure to talk about these feelings and why you are having them.

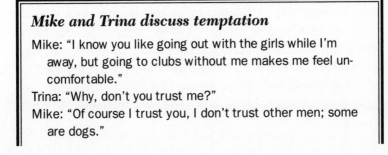

Mike and Trina discuss temptation

Mike: "I know you like going out with the girls while I'm away, but going to clubs without me makes me feel uncomfortable."

Trina: "Why, don't you trust me?"

Mike: "Of course I trust you, I don't trust other men; some are dogs."

Trina: "Well, what do you expect me to do for a whole year
while you're away?"

Mike: "Going to movies, out to eat, places with the kids
seem harmless. Some men will look at you being at a
club and automatically think you want to be picked up."

Trina: "Well, I guess going to the club without you is probably not smart. Don't worry about me clubbing, you just
come home so we can go together."

When your loved one is going to be away for an extended
amount of time, your negative thoughts can take over. Instead of
filling your mind with love and anticipation for your reunion,
you fill your mind with doubts about your partner's faithfulness.
Before you know it, you're sending vibes over the phone that
you're angry or suspicious. Tell me if that doesn't put a damper
on a homecoming! Many of us who live in long-distance relationships find ourselves in this predicament at one time or another.
It's important to remember that we can choose what we allow
our minds to think. Instead of filling our thoughts with, "I deserve to go out and dance if I want to," you should be thinking
"Mike would be so hurt if he knew I was out clubbing without
him. In reality, I'm not missing anything, anyway."

To begin, we must first look inward and become conscious of
how we spend our time. In long-distance relationships, we often
seek out friendships with others who are, or have been, in similar situations. Our good intentions of sharing experiences, fears,
hopes, and loneliness, however, are in danger of drowning in a
sea of despair. The friends we choose have a powerful impact on
our thoughts and feelings, so we must be very cautious when deciding with whom to share our innermost thoughts and emotions.

THE IMPORTANCE OF POSITIVE INFLUENCES

One night I was eating dinner with a co-worker during our patrol shift, and I discussed my husband's duty in Korea and how much I missed him. Out of the blue, my co-worker asked me if I ever thought about my husband cheating on me. Shocked, but without hesitation, I quickly stated in a stern voice, "My husband has never given me a reason to think that he would cheat on me, and I wholeheartedly trust him." My co-worker replied that most of the men he knew, including himself, had had an extramarital affair at one time or another, and he asked why I thought my husband would be any different, especially while he's away for a year in Korea. Still shocked that my co-worker would say this, I told him I refused to believe my husband would do something like that, and I changed the subject.

Although I escaped the conversation, what really hurt were the thoughts I had to endure later when I was at home and had time to think about what he had said. I know, from the many people I've met and worked with over the years, that adultery is alive and well. It's all over the newspapers and headlines when someone famous is caught. So now I was faced with a question that seemed to play over and over in my mind, "Why is my husband any different?" From that night on, my misgivings about my husband's fidelity never seemed to leave my mind. I'd tell myself that I knew my husband had very high morals and respect for our marriage. I knew I trusted my husband, but, nevertheless, that conversation with my co-worker stuck in my mind. I found myself feeling angry, hurt, and sometimes doubtful. I know many of you will ask yourselves the same question.

Many friends I've discussed these thoughts with have suggested that the best way to avoid these doubts and fears during the time of separation is to surround yourself with friends who have loving, working, and positive relationships.

Ann talks about fidelity

My friend Ann told me that Lisa couldn't wait until her husband left town so she could go out and do what she wanted. The two had been friends in the past, but now that Ann knew her friend was probably committing adultery every time her husband left town, she decided she didn't want any part of that friendship. Ann told me she did not want to get caught up in the lies. Ann later told me she was tempted to "just go out" with her friend, but when she thought about it, she knew she didn't belong with a friend who didn't have the same values and respect for her marriage that she did. I couldn't agree more.

That was a good warning for Ann and me to stay away from "friends" like that, especially during a long separation. Time and time again friends tell me how they were talked into going out with some of these so-called friends and how it ended with regret. Don't get me wrong, everyone is entitled to go out, have a good time, and unwind, but you have to feel good about yourself the next day and in no way harm your relationship. If you're like many, subjecting yourself to temptation is often a dangerous game, particularly for young marriages. You're the only one who knows what temptations you can and can't withstand.

When my husband was away for the one-year tour of Korea, I decided that if our six-year-old son couldn't accompany me wherever I went during that year, then I probably didn't need to be there myself. I didn't know what to expect from myself during a one-year separation—we had never been away from each other for that long. I was somewhat scared this might be the end of our then seven-year marriage. I told several friends that this Korea tour would either make us or break us. I feel that if anyone can take a one-year-separation tour of Korea or combat and come out with a more loving relationship than before, then we can make it through anything. I stuck to the promise of not going anyplace where our young son wouldn't be welcomed, and my relationship survived and grew stronger that year.

I thought this promise would be hard for me to keep, but I found it was quite easy. I knew there was nothing out there that I was missing, and that thought seemed to give me a feeling of peace. If I am at peace with myself, then I can handle anything that can go wrong. I know if things had turned out differently and if our marriage didn't survive that year, I would still have felt good about myself knowing I had done everything I could to make our relationship work. Otherwise, I would have to go through life wondering if I had caused it to turn sour.

We all choose what thoughts we want to live with, and we make our own decisions whether to take action on those thoughts. I made a commitment to be true and faithful and see if this love stuff really works—and it does!

When families face long deployments, I try to assure them their time apart can make the relationship better and more meaningful. Sometimes it may be the end to what was already a failing relationship.

More times than not, the relationship grows stronger, and they reunite with a newfound appreciation and love for each other and their families. Trying to convince someone that his or her relationship may actually improve at the beginning of a long deployment is difficult, but time always tells. It may start with hearing a different tune in your loved one's voice, a sweet unexpected love letter, or hearing for the first time, "I really miss home and the kids." A feeling of forgiveness for all the past disagreements or heartaches starts to sink in, and both of you realize that you have something special and worth fighting for. You'll then be on your way to a whole new beginning in your long-distance relationship. It's a great accomplishment, and it's one you can always look back on and gain strength from.

TELLTALE SIGNS

Some spouses have told me about their unfortunate experiences with their loved ones at home or away who started behaving very strangely and the uneasy feeling that overcame them. Through my discussions with friends who have been down this path, I've made a list of some of the most obvious signs to be aware of if you feel concerned that your loved one is involved with another, either on deployment or at home.

- ★ Appearing bored with you and life in general
- ★ Refusing to discuss sexual desire, even in phone conversations when on deployment
- ★ Lying and telling you conflicting stories both at home and away
- ★ Spending more money than usual
- ★ Wanting to go out with "the gang" more than usual
- ★ Staying out later each time
- ★ Working longer hours
- ★ Unwilling to have a conversation, and getting angry over trivialities, especially on the phone
- ★ Abandoning religious faith
- ★ Telephoning/e-mailing less often

All these things can happen in a loving relationship, but usually at different times or for specific reasons.

Sherri told me, "You don't just wake up one morning and think to yourself, gee, my husband might be having an affair, and you have reasons to think that he is." It's a gradual process of accumulated details.

What now? Do you confront your mate, or do you suffer these doubts that consume you every minute of every day? When you take all this and add distance and time, the dilemma

only magnifies. You have to learn to explain your perspective so
your loved one can see it as you do. Be very careful not to accuse
your partner of something that may not be true. False accusa-
tions will only cause defensive reactions and things can blow up.
Paint your partner a picture—describe what you are feeling,
seeing, or hearing and how your spouse would react if you were
doing the same things.

It may sound hard. The key is to have this conversation with
all the love you can muster up and in a quiet, concerned voice.
Don't be accusatory; you have to get over the urge to scream, "I
know you're having an affair." Your whole life may change during this conversation. Fill your mind with all the reasons you
love your partner. Write down all his or her good qualities—all
the reasons why you fell in love in the first place.

Sit down together when you won't be distracted, and tell your
spouse how much you love him or her. When your love and appreciation are clear, state what your concerns are and why you
have them. Describe how you see your relationship. Just flat out
ask if there's any love for you anymore. Ask, "Are you having an
affair?" It's very hard for someone to tell a lie straight to your
face without showing obvious signs. Liars will often become
very defensive, tiptoe around answers, or avoid answering the
question altogether. They'll often want to change the subject or
will become nervous and blame you or others for the problem.

Where this conversation goes from here is up to you. If you
allow yourself to become loud or accusing, the scene will probably
end in a negative way. If you show true concern about how your
relationship should be and how you want to be the best wife, husband, girlfriend, or boyfriend possible, you will gain more insight.
Some issues may come out of this conversation that you are not
aware of. You need to prepare yourself mentally to accept what
you may not want to hear or what you may need to hear.

I know this is something that we all dread, but ask yourself,
which is worse, going through every day with thoughts of your

spouse involved with infidelity or knowing the truth? The old saying still stands, "The truth shall set you free." Some of us are unsure at this point if we're willing to hear the truth, and that's why this conversation may never take place. Some of us don't want to know. That is a decision that only you can make. Many of us can resolve these unwanted feelings or concerns if we only take the chance to ask the questions whose answers we fear the most. Although to set ourselves up for what may turn out as a huge disappointment is hard, we often reap more love and understanding within our relationship that we thought wasn't there to begin with just from being honest with each other.

Sherri's experience with infidelity in a letter

"Let him who is free from sin cast the first stone. I may not have committed the same sins, but that certainly does not free me from any guilt.

"It takes two people to make a happy marriage. I feel that I could have made better choices, that could have changed his decision to have an affair, such as not work-ing such long hours and making a warm, loving environ-ment at home so that he would want to be with me and only me.

"It takes two to make a good marriage and two to have an affair. Please don't think that this lessens the fact that he made the final decision to cheat. I take no responsibil-ity for that.

"When I finally got the truth out of him, I had known for a couple of months. So I was ready to hear the truth and move on, either on my own or as a family. When I heard the truth, I simply asked, 'Where do we go from here?' My answer came to me. . . . We go on; we build on this weak-ness. We take this bad time, and we make our lives bet-ter. We have done that. He told me the entire truth,

and said he just never realized, until our conversation,
how much I really do love him.

"It didn't take me long to get over this episode. I'm not
sure why, but I have a very strong personality. Maybe that
helped me in a different way.

"I have never been a jealous person, nor have I let this
incident make me so. I guess it was all about learning
to forgive and starting over. I think it's something every
couple should be able to say and mean it wholeheartedly.
I will tell you something I told him in the midst of all of
this growing and rebuilding . . . , 'I love you more today
than I did yesterday, and I know I am going to love you
more tomorrow than I do today.'"

I admire her strength and their commitment to work things
out. This letter makes a statement: Love truly has no bound-
aries.

A FLING OR AN AFFAIR?

If you had to choose which situation is the worse of these two
evils, which one would it be? I understand a fling as a "one night
stand" or a short-term "sex only" relationship. An affair, on the
other hand, is more like a meaningful relationship in which each
partner shares more than *just* sex. It involves more emotions
and plans for a long-term relationship, along with many lies and
deceits. And would you, or could you, forgive your loved one for
having either a fling or an affair? If you're in this predicament,
you may want to ask yourself this question before you bring up
the subject.

This is a personal matter. For instance, if your relationship is
young and you find out your loved one has been unfaithful, you

may want to end it. The more time we have invested in our relationships, the harder it seems to let go. When children are involved it gets even worse. I have known of women who have taken their men back after learning of an affair, and all seemed to work out. But I have also heard that once the trust is broken, it's rarely regained and then not as fully as before. What each of us can or are willing to handle emotionally is as different as night and day.

If your loved one has given you more than enough reason to believe that he or she may be having just sex or a full-blown affair, then it's time to talk. It is very hard to deal with this situation over the phone, in letters, or in e-mails, so you should wait until you are together again, if possible. You need to have a conversation in which you can look each other in the eye and try to make the best decisions for you and your family. If your loved one wants to end it, then at least make him or her do it face to face.

One common mistake is that we try to have these conversations in passing. We often don't take the time to sit down in an uninterrupted environment to discuss what may be the most important issues in our lives. Maybe it's because of the emotions we're scared will surface. Or maybe we know we will get angry, and we want to be able to end the conversation easily if it becomes too heated. I think we are only taking half the dosage schedule penicillin if we do this. The problems may disappear for a while, but will soon return with greater strength. Swallow that pride and fear, and take the time to get your love life in order. If you don't take the risk, you may never get over this hurdle.

Is your relationship worth saving?

I'm not saying every relationship is worth saving. Some relationships need to end. But if you think it's worth saving, then it probably is. It will require your willingness to take that chance from time to time to get some hard questions answered. This may gradually get easier. As you work on your communication skills, talking and sharing your feelings will get easier over time. Most women seem to feel freer to talk about their feelings than men do. Women need to understand this and allow men to grow in their communication skills. Try to help your loved ones become more open with feelings they may often keep hidden.

If you know, whether in your heart or through hard evidence, that your loved one has committed adultery, the next question is, "Do I stick it out or just leave the relationship?" We've all heard time and time again that you shouldn't stay in a relationship just for the sake of your kids. Yet, this is the main reason why many stay in troubled marriages. Somewhere along the line, the love for our child or children comes first, and many spouses sacrifice their own happiness so that the children can be happy. Every case will be different, and only you know if your kids are happy or not. Don't fool yourself into thinking that kids don't pick up on tension between Mom and Dad.

Finances, parents, and religion are other reasons couples stay together. The list can go on and on. No right answer is available, and we are the ones who have to live in the relationships we choose. Some people who have stuck it out find this path worth it, and they are glad they did. Some who choose to end their relationships go on to find happiness with other partners. I can offer you insight from a group of people who have been through this kind of thing.

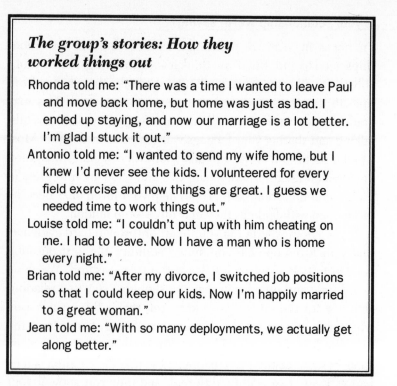

The group's stories: How they worked things out

Rhonda told me: "There was a time I wanted to leave Paul and move back home, but home was just as bad. I ended up staying, and now our marriage is a lot better. I'm glad I stuck it out."

Antonio told me: "I wanted to send my wife home, but I knew I'd never see the kids. I volunteered for every field exercise and now things are great. I guess we needed time to work things out."

Louise told me: "I couldn't put up with him cheating on me. I had to leave. Now I have a man who is home every night."

Brian told me: "After my divorce, I switched job positions so that I could keep our kids. Now I'm happily married to a great woman."

Jean told me: "With so many deployments, we actually get along better."

There is one exception. I'll never agree to encourage anyone to stay in an abusive relationship. Abuse, whether physical or verbal or both, hurts not only the partner but also the kids. If you feel that you're in this type of relationship, don't hesitate to talk with a professional and find out your options.

KISS AND TELL

Have you ever heard a friend confess to a one-night stand or long-term affair? You will know that in the end most who have cheated are full of guilt and shame and are scared to death they are going to lose their marriage or relationship. Maybe you are the one who is wondering, do I tell my partner?

I've received mixed views on this, but the most common answer is "Yes." As hard as you think it will be, tell your partner and see if you can work it out. Flings and affairs are often the outcome of other issues in the marriage that we didn't deal with at the time. Oftentimes, after a cleansing of the soul through honesty, you'll find out the root of the problem.

If more couples would seek professional help before allowing these problems to get out of control, many marriages could be saved. Most military installations offer free marriage counseling through the chaplain services. You could also obtain marriage counseling through Military OneSource. Even if your spouse is not available or won't go, you will benefit from seeking guidance. The resources are available, but more of us should swallow our pride and seek it out. Marriage is hard enough, and the added stress of military life only multiplies the hardship.

Many service members are under the misconception that seeking marriage counseling will hinder their careers. Most commanders and supervisors know that if the service member is happily married, then he or she will be an asset to the unit. The opposite is also true if there are family issues at home, especially during deployments, because the service member and his family issues can become a burden on the unit. Worse case, the service member may become careless by putting himself and his teammates in greater danger from lack of focus.

Love is a commitment

To "feel" in love is great, but those feelings can be swept away into the morning trash. Love is not just a feeling, but a commitment. People use the excuse that being apart from each other caused them to have an affair. Look deeper, and you'll see that being apart is just one piece of the puzzle. Many couples are away from each other for long periods and remain faithful and committed, so obviously, separation doesn't need to lead to infidelity.

As mentioned earlier, I know of relationships that have survived one or both partners having affairs or flings, but the trust is never quite the same. Larry, my past co-worker who has been down this road, lives with constant interrogation from his wife, who doesn't trust him as far as she can throw him. Even though his days of running around are long over, his wife lives in constant fear it will happen again. She never trusts him around any woman, no matter how old or young. I feel sorry for her and the pain she lives with. Partners need to realize that having a fling or an affair not only affects their short-term desires but can even affect your whole family forever.

CHAPLAIN S'S ANALOGY ON PREVENTING INFIDELITY

Our chaplain, during marriage enrichment training, used two illustrations that reflect the difference between a man and a woman when it comes to sensuality and sexuality. Understanding these differences and satisfying the spouse is one of many measures in preventing infidelity.

As a man, imagine that your wife possesses two pitchers, one a sensual pitcher, and the second a sexual pitcher. Within the marriage relationship, men do many things to fill that sensual pitcher. Each time you speak to your wife in ways that show her appreciation, it is like pouring a little water into her sensual pitcher. When you complete your shopping at that convenience store, and remember your wife's love for chocolate and purchase her the good stuff, it is like pouring a little water into her sensual pitcher. When you leave work early, just so that you can go home and spend quality time with her, it is like pouring water into her sensual pitcher. As you buy her that small gift when it is not her birthday, or tell her how beautiful she is, you fill her sensual pitcher. Over time, that sensual pitcher will become completely full and will overflow into another pitcher called the sexual pitcher. As more and more water overflows into the sexual pitcher, your wife's desire for sex will naturally increase. One of the husband's many responsibilities in the marriage is to fill his wife's sensual pitcher until it is over-flowing.

As a woman, imagine walking for many hours through a very hot desert without any water. After only a short amount of time, you become thirsty. After a few hours you feel as if you are dying of thirst. Continuing to walk, your mind betrays you and you begin to feel that you will not survive, but in the distance there is someone. Walking closer to this person, you realize that it is your husband and he is drink-ing a glass of cold water. You feel relieved and ask him for a drink of his water, but rather than giving you a drink, he turns his back to you and walks away. Ladies, sex for your husband is just like that glass of cold water. Each time you resist your husband's advances for sex, rolling over, turning your back to him, it is just like refusing him water in a hot desert. One of the wife's responsibilities in the marriage is to give her husband a regular drink of that water.

I have never heard of this before, but it makes good sense to me! As I listened to these illustrations, I thought of how helpful this concept can be in preventing infidelity. It is often the case that a woman has affairs with men from her workplace. It is these men in the workplace whom she allows to speak to her words of appreciation, buy her cards or small gifts, and even tell her how beautiful she is to them. The reason a woman some-times chooses to have a sexual relationship with these men is be-cause they have filled her sensual pitcher, and it has overflowed into her sexual pitcher. At the same time, if the husband (after filling his wife's sensual pitcher) comes to her for a drink and she continues to turn him away, like a nomad in the desert, he will often seek a drink from someone else. There are other women who seek to pour out their water to give the thirsty husband just what he needs to quench his thirst.

Ladies, get out your sensual pitchers, and, husbands, start filling! Just remember . . . he's already thirsty for that glass of water!

★ ★ ★

TIPS TO REMEMBER

1. Do not test your relationship with infidelity.
2. Set aside time before the deployment to discuss fidelity in your relationship if this is on your mind.
3. Hang around with friends who are at the same level as or higher in a relationship than you are. Iron sharpens iron!
4. Be confident that time apart will often make the relationship stronger and more meaningful.
5. Decide which is worse: knowing or not knowing the truth.
6. Remember, love is not just an emotion, but loyalty and a vow.
7. Remember, if you believe your marriage is worth the effort to save, then it probably is.
8. Seek counseling. Many resources are available to help. Do not hesitate to talk with a professional.
9. Do not kid yourself, when tension exists between Mom and Dad, children can feel it.
10. Attend marriage retreats.

Chapter 5

CHILDREN

WE ALL HAVE OUR WAYS of dealing with our loved ones being away, but what about the children? When separated from one or both of their parents they too have their own ways of showing their fear, anxiety, anger, loss, confusion, and frustration. If we can learn to recognize the children's need for adapting, as we have our own, then we are better equipped to help them get through it. When we help our children deal with the absence of Mom or Dad, we also help ourselves. If the child is happy, the parents are happy.

HANDLING ADJUSTMENT

All children, regardless of age, go through some type of adjustment phase when a parent leaves home. Some children want a few days to be alone, some children need to stay busy and not dwell on Mom's or Dad's absence, and some worry themselves sick. We just have to realize that our children share the same emotions we do, but they may show them in a different way. Pay attention to how the child behaves after the departure, and then help that child get through it based on his or her individual reaction.

If your child stays at a sitter for long hours, ask the sitter how she thinks your child is getting along. Many spouses will call each other more often during the deployment for consolation.

Remember, you are your children's best friend, and they need consolation just as much as you do.

Now, we've done all the right things to prepare our children for an upcoming deployment or trip. We've talked about it and answered all their questions. Then the big day comes, Mom or Dad leaves, and it starts—the mood swings, the teary eyes, the back talk, the tantrums, and a vast array of other emotional reactions. Some children become withdrawn and refuse to talk about it. Others may have outbursts or tantrums. We need to realize that some of our children's erratic behavior is their way of showing how much they miss Mom or Dad. We can't take it personally or allow ourselves to react negatively to their actions, and thus we must become tolerant of a child's outbursts.

We're often left feeling helpless and don't know which would be best—to leave them alone or to try to talk with them about it. Many of us don't have a schedule that allows us to spend as much time as we'd like trying to get to the bottom of what is bothering our children. We know the root of the problem is the other parent's absence, but do we take time to wonder what our children are going through? I know from experience how hard it is to become a temporarily single parent, but you mustn't forget the thoughts of your children and the feelings they have because Mom or Dad is away.

The hardest moments, especially for children, are soon after the deployment and soon after the return. These are the "readjusting phases." The first days, and even the first hours, after deployment everyone begins to adjust to a new routine. We all know children like routine, and when things change, they are easily upset. In the first chapter I discussed the strategy of creating a diversion on deployment day, but you can't live in a constant state of diversion, and neither can your children. Both you and I want our children to be just as happy with their new routine as they were when the whole family was together.

I am not a child behavior expert, but I am a mother and have many friends who have shared their stories with me. The earlier we establish the new routine and the more consistent it is, the easier it is to for the child to adapt to the separation. If you are working, chances are you will likely have to make some changes. Try to stick to these changes, even though your new schedule may be completely different from when both of you were home, developing a new routine quickly will be a comfort to your children.

Common routine changes children go through during deployments

★ Staying later at an after-school program

★ Eating fewer home-cooked meals or not keeping a regular dinnertime

★ Spending time at a babysitter's on weekends

★ Attending more outings

DISCIPLINE

Once you've established the new routine, allow time for behaviors to adjust. Be as patient and forgiving as possible. Most of all show an abundance of love for your children. Make sure they know that they are the most important part of your life and that you'll all make the best of the time Mom or Dad is away.

I'm not saying you should let the children run wild. Find a happy medium. If you are too lax, you may make them dread when Dad gets home. The last thing you want is to make either parent the disciplinarian—discipline always should be a shared responsibility. If you're not clear about the rules, then the children will take advantage of that.

> ## Cathy's view of discipline
>
> "Time, a little more patience, and staying busy works best for us. I let them know that just because their dad is away does not mean the rules of behavior have changed. When they realize that things are going to stay the same as much as possible, they usually settle back down."

COPING SKILLS

Here are some ways to help children cope with deployment:

★ Tell your children about deployments together, and answer any questions they might have.

★ Have the departing parent make a recording of him or her reading a favorite story to the children. Young children will find this comforting at bedtime.

★ Provide the departing parent with items that will make it easier to send tapes, letters, and photos back to the children while he or she is on deployment. It may be hard to obtain some of these items once out of the country.

★ Do not vent where the children can overhear your fears or frustrations; they might adopt them as their own.

★ Explain to them why Dad or Mom is going away in positive terms they can understand. Children will often blame themselves or become angry at the military.

★ Show your children maps and other information about the country where Mom or Dad is on deployment and what the military is doing for the people there.

★ Do not allow your children to watch negative media coverage of war and especially service members losing their lives. This kind of news is hard to stomach and may cause sleepless nights.

★ Make sure the spouse at home keeps a positive attitude so that the children will feel secure.

★ Plan and talk about fun things you will do with the children.

★ Plan and talk about the fun things you are going to do as a family when Mom or Dad returns.

If your child begins to misbehave on an extreme level around the time of deployment, then it's time to have a heart-to-heart. If he or she is a teenager, delaying this talk will only increase the distance between you. If you can't find a way to have a conversation with your child, then find someone who can help the two of you make that connection, whether or not it is a close friend or family member or a counselor. You will risk losing your child if you don't find a way to communicate. How many of us know our children as well as we would like to? We are the adults, and responsible for taking the extra time, effort, and patience to get to know our children.

Maggie's story

My friend Maggie, who's endured several deployments, told me that after the first deployment her youngest son was frightened when his dad returned and it took their son many days to warm up to him again. Not only was this stressful on the child, but it was heartbreaking for the dad. The next deployment she video recorded her husband reading books to the kids. She made several recordings and told me her children loved watching and hearing their dad read them stories during the deployment. The homecoming following this deployment went much better and she feels the homemade videos made all the difference.

> The USO sponsors the United Through Reading program and has sites In Iraq, Afghanistan, and other theaters, as well as stateside installations to help promote this sort of connection between children and their deployed parents. They video the service member reading the book, and send the book and DVD to the child's home.

Teens

Teenagers can be impossible to deal with, but we as parents must find a way to relate to our children, no matter how difficult that may be. Many teens tell me that their parents don't know who their friends are or even who they are. In their eyes, parents spend too much time being at work, talking on the phone, working out at the gym, doing housework, preparing meals, and doing other things that take our attention away from them.

Ask yourself how much time you set aside for your children, you may surprised. The older the child becomes, the more he or she figures out how much time we are wasting that could be spent with them. Teenagers often hold grudges without even being aware of it. We shouldn't chalk up a teen's bad behavior to attitude—it more likely indicates an unspoken need for more attention, affection, and love.

The bottom line is that they want our time. They want our attention, our approval, our respect, and our affection. Many par-

> "There is more hunger for love and appreciation in this world than for bread."
>
> **—Mother Teresa**

ents are so caught up with themselves that their children start feeling they are not wanted, understood, or even loved. Many of the teens are filling a void they feel is missing in their lives. They will try to fill these needs, and what they find can sometimes be dangerous. Drugs, sex, mature video games, and alcohol are just a few of the most common concerns. We can't point to the kids up the street, the bad influence at school, or our loved one's absence as the single cause of our teens' behaviors. A combination of many things causes problems. We may not be able to fix them all, but we can help our kids if we take the time to work on one piece of the problem at a time.

Difficult children

With all that's just been said/written, I understand it's not always just basic child-rearing issues. I read that surveys say 20 percent of American parents report having a child at home who is so difficult it is almost impossible to lead a normal life. Most of us would not put it so strongly, but it's plainly true that some children are harder to raise than others. There are a ton of books on raising children and many are geared for the difficult child. It's up to you as the parent to educate yourself on these issues, and by all means seek professional help if it gets to that point.

One family did all the right things, but no matter how hard they tried, how many counselors they took their child to, he was determined to remain rebellious. They have four other children who are doing fine. You can't always blame yourself for your child's out-of-control behavior. Our society does, and that's why when these things happen, many families keep it secret. We are all afraid of being judged harshly. Regardless, some issues cannot be ignored and need to be dealt with. Their son no longer lives in their home. As sad and heartbreaking as it was for the parents, they also knew and wanted to do what was best for the entire family.

Coping with short deployments

Unfortunately, short deployments can be just as hard on children as long ones. Many youngsters have no concept of time—to them, a week might as well be a month or a year. For example, with my husband still stationed at Ft. Bragg, North Carolina, my son and I moved to Savannah, Georgia, early so that my son could attend one school and not have to move in the middle of the school year. My husband was still able to visit on the weekends. At first I thought we were lucky to be able to see each other most weekends, but I was wrong. Our nine-year-old son went through separation anxiety every week. I, too, felt depressed and lonely every Sunday when my husband would drive away. I still wanted my husband to return the next weekend, but I was tired of putting my son and me through this on a weekly basis.

Maria's story

For long deployments, "we take poster board and make up monthly calendars. We mark on the calendar all the major holidays, birthdays, anniversaries, church picnics, camping trips, and anything that represents a mini celebration. Then we live from celebration to celebration. The children take turns crossing off the days. When you are looking forward in time, it is easy to see a short distance, that is, a week, as opposed to a year. The next thing you know, we are looking at Daddy's Return."

SCHOOLWORK AND BEHAVIOR

Perhaps a few weeks, or even months, after your spouse is away, you'll receive a letter from school about failing grades or outbursts of anger in class. Just when you thought the deployment was going smoothly, and everyone seemed to be so well adjusted, you discover problems are brewing just beneath the surface. If problems like these aren't handled quickly, an excellent student can become a failing student or a troublemaker.

Problems in school are another expression of children's frustrations, and parents need to be aware of them. Become proactive and talk with the teacher before any other problems arise. Let the teacher know the child's dad or mom is away, and tell them for how long. If the child has had problems in the past dealing with his or her parent's deployments, tell the teacher and relate some of your strategies for helping your child through this tough time.

Strategies for teachers and parents to help children cope

★ Get the whole class involved in where the child's mom or dad is on deployment.

★ Encourage the parents to bring in articles from that country or food items.

★ Ask the class to write letters to the deployed child's mom or dad or others serving with the parent.

★ Make the deployed service member's unit a class project.

★ Make the deployed unit an American flag from the imprint of the children's painted hands.

★ Have the class study that part of the world.

★ Have the deployed service member send photos or a video to where he or she is stationed.

★ Invite the service member to the class once he or she returns. Have him or her talk to the class and display some of the equipment used. Let the kids have hands-on time with the items.

Even if the child has not had problems in the past, let the teacher know about your spouse's absence. (Special Operations spouses may not have this luxury.) Lynn told me her child never had a problem until he was eight years old, and she was shocked when the teacher contacted her. Sometimes a teacher can be a big help with your child's adjustment and can help you prevent problems before the grades drop. Always take the time to be aware of your child's schoolwork and school life.

WHEN THE SADNESS WILL NOT GO AWAY

Younger children who don't yet understand time are often doubtful that Mom or Dad will return. My friend Robin told me her four-year-old was still crying and missing Daddy after he had been away for a month. Nothing seemed to cheer him up and Robin was heartbroken, but Robin was patient. Ultimately, her four-year-old did get past this phase. This feeling is hard to explain unless you've been there and looked into those tear-filled eyes while trying your best to make everything better.

Often, a spouse who is away doesn't fully understand what his or her children go through and what the partner left behind must contend with.

If you cannot help your child overcome his or her sadness, get some sort of help—it could be more than just "the blues."

Warning signs of potential problems

★ Behavioral changes—many become withdrawn, short tempered, and tearful.

★ Sleep disturbance—difficulty falling asleep, too much or too little, nightmares.

★ Frequent headaches or stomachaches.

★ Behavioral problems—at school, at home, or with other kids.

★ Appetite changes—weight loss or gain.

The military provides free counseling to children as well as spouses. You are responsible for getting the help he or she needs. Parents don't have all the answers, and seeking professional help isn't a sign of weakness but rather of conscientious parenting.

Sometimes our children miss the absent parent more than usual, and in these moments, remember to be extra patient, gentle, and loving. When you or I have "one of those days," we pick up the phone and call our favorite confidante or e-mail a long-distance friend who knows us better than anyone else. You must be that person for your child. Don't always wait for your child to come to you. Ask your child if he or she is missing Dad or Mom. Let the child know it is completely normal to be lonely without the parent or frightened for the parent. Always reassure your children. Get into the practice of consoling your children while they are young, because you will need to know how to do it when they are teenagers.

WHEN THE SERVICE MEMBER RETURNS

Mom or Dad's return can often be almost as difficult for children as deployment was. The family has been short a member for anywhere from a week to a year or more and has settled into some sort of routine. When you announce to the children that Mom or Dad will be back in a few days, another readjustment starts! Fortunately, this readjustment is usually easier and more pleasant than when Mom or Dad left. Your children are as excited as you are, so be patient, bend some rules, and give your children some extra attention, just as you did during week one. Things will be back to normal before you know it.

★ ★ ★

TIPS TO REMEMBER

1. Be aware that every child has a different way of showing his or her emotion, be it fear, anxiety, anger, or another, and these emotions can often manifest themselves in bad behavior.
2. Make time to console your child.
3. Find a way to have a conversation with your child, or find someone who can help.
4. Give your child your time and attention.
5. Take note that both short and long deployments can be difficult for children—and for you!
6. Pay attention to warning signs of depression or stress.
7. Get help if you cannot assist your child to overcome sadness.
8. Do not wait for your child to come to you for help.
9. Try to be as patient, gentle, and loving to your children as you can during this time, especially just after your spouse's deployment and return.
10. Some of the hardest moments are soon after the deployment and soon after the return.
11. Make videos of the deployed spouse reading children's stories.

Chapter 6

CAREER

FOR MILITARY SPOUSES, having a steady career is nearly impossible. Some of us don't mind changing jobs with each move we have to make. We may just want to supplement our incomes in order to have a little extra for the family, without a full-time commitment. Keep in mind that each new place will offer different employment opportunities.

Think of your long-term goals, and choose your career wisely so that you don't have to start over every time you move. I know from experience how hard it is to think of all these aspects when you are young, but with planning a little, you can have a successful career while living the life of a devoted military spouse and dedicated parent.

Those who choose to pursue a career and maintain a military marriage know what a challenge this is. When the moves take us far from home, family, and friends, it can be even more daunting. If we make long-range plans, we can make better decisions about navigating a career.

When you're taking care of the kids while your spouse is away, your life is much like that of a single parent. Family responsibilities often stand in the way of career growth. This chapter addresses a few issues for military spouses to consider when choosing a career.

SICK LEAVE

When acting as a single parent during deployments, you must not only count on having your own sick days but also take sick days when your children are ill. Along with illness, you'll also need time off to take them to regular checkups and school activities. For military spouses with two or more children, these responsibilities can interfere significantly with your work schedule. If you're fortunate, your boss may be sympathetic to your predicament and adjust your schedule to fit your needs. Be aware that frequent absences may not be forgotten when it comes time for performance evaluations or promotion recommendations. Even if you're lucky enough to have a supervisor that understands your situation, you may have co-workers who resent what they see as special treatment. This misperception can lead to tension between you and your fellow employees, who may find it hard if not impossible to understand your military lifestyle.

Dawn told me that either her supervisor or co-workers have asked her on several occasions, "Why can't your husband take your child to the doctor once in a while?" Or, "Why can't your husband stay home with the kids sometimes when they are sick?" For some reason, the kids just never seem to get sick when the service member is home. The idea of a service member calling in to tell his or her commander that he or she is staying home with the kids, is usually out of the question, and this circumstance is clearly impossible when he or she is on deployment. Dawn often felt resentment toward these types of comments, and they only added to the multiple stresses of dealing with a sick child, missing work, and having her husband deployed into combat. If this happens to you, remember, most of the time our civilian counterparts don't mean any harm, they just can't understand what we're going through.

DAY CARE DILEMMA

When we first moved to Ft. Bragg, North Carolina, I decided to go back to work and was dumbfounded at the lack of twenty-four-hour child-care facilities (my work hours were not 9–5). After all, Ft. Bragg was the Home of the Airborne and Special Operations Forces, on call twenty-four hours a day, seven days a week, and 365 days a year! I thought finding day care would be no problem. I did find one twenty-four-hour day care listed in the Yellow Pages, but when I went by, I didn't bother to get out of the car. (First impressions are important!) I found myself limited to working jobs that didn't run past 5:30 P.M. so that I could make it to day care by 6 P.M. Because I had no friends or family in town who could watch my child, I was very frustrated.

My husband was away increasingly more often during that time, so I was frantic to find a sitter, one who wouldn't quit because of my unpredictable work schedule. Finally, I found someone whom I could trust to watch our son in her home while I worked. At the time, I was working as a deputy sheriff, with long hours at night, on weekends, and some holidays, not to mention occupational hazards.

By the time we finally moved from Ft. Bragg, I had obtained five pay raises, a rewarding position in the detective division, and a schedule that allowed me to work mostly days. When I called to inquire about obtaining a similar position in law enforcement at our next duty station, I was told that I would most likely have to start over as a road patrol officer with 24/7 rotating hours. Because most states require their specific state certification as a qualification to work in law enforcement in their specific state, I would also have to start at the bottom of the pay scale. In the end, I decided it wasn't worth it to my family or me. I can't say I wasted my years as a deputy sheriff in North Carolina, but I definitely went through a lot of undue stress and frustration because of that career choice.

PROMOTIONAL OPPORTUNITIES FOR
MILITARY SPOUSES

I'll never forget the time I was facing a promotion board, and one of the senior board members asked me how my husband's military career affected how long I'd stay in the area. I answered the question honestly and said, "Should my husband receive orders to change duty stations, my family would move." I know employers must look out for the interest of the organization and spend their time and resources on training individuals who will later be of value to them, but I couldn't help being disappointed. I later asked others who were seeking the same promotion if they had been asked that question, and the answer was a unanimous "No." I knew then that my position as a military spouse would probably hinder my chances for promotion.

After losing the chance for advancement in my career, I began to understand why they grant military spouses half the service member's retirement benefits even if the couple divorces after at least ten years of marriage. The frequent moves required of a military career make it difficult for any spouse of a service member to build a career—or a pension—anywhere. This issue is only part of the enormous requirement of military spouses. I admire the men and women who have been willing to give up a chance at having a long-term career as well as the security of a retirement because of their commitment to a service member. I know some people like me who are career oriented struggle with this. If you are, then be careful because it could come between you and your marriage.

Some careers will transfer from state to state, but you will often have to start back at the bottom of the totem pole. Wilma despaired, "I find that you always have to start over at the bottom or close to it with each move, so it feels like you are never getting anywhere."

Giny's Constant Seniority Loss

My friend Giny, who's a nurse, said she would lose her hard-earned seniority every time she moved. She had to work late shifts or weekends until she could build up her seniority again. Even though she often had more experience than most of the other nurses, she was stuck with the hours no one else wanted because she was new.

Finding a career that's compatible with your lifestyle

You may feel you have to settle for some unfulfilling, boring, mediocre job just because you're a military spouse and you move from one location to another. I was beginning to think that myself. One day I attended a workshop called "Follow Your Dreams While You Follow the Military." The workshop was a blast and the founders/authors, Kathie Hightower and Holly Scherer, were inspirational in their delivery. Little did they know, I was too embarrassed to speak up in the class, but I too had a dream! I feel they had an impact on me that day and helped me to gain the confidence to try to reach for my little dream (writing a book). Now they travel worldwide conducting their workshops and are the authors of *Help! I'm a Military Spouse—I Get a Life Too!* Their book is not only about finding a career, but full of wonderful guidance on how to live your best life while being a military spouse. Look for their upcoming new edition, with a new title.

I don't want to list a lot of books because there are just too many great ones to list them all. However . . . when it comes to finding a job and making career choices one book seems to stand out. That book is titled *What Color Is Your Parachute? A Practical Manual for Job-Hunters and Career-Changers*. It is described on the cover as "the best-selling job-hunting and career-changing book in the world. Twenty thousand people buy the book each month, and there are more than 8 million copies in print. In its lifetime, it has been on the *New York Times* Best-Seller List (paperback) a total of 288 weeks."

I hesitate listing websites as they always seem to change, but since you have the titles, you should have no problem finding these books and their websites. Many of us are still searching what we want to be when we grow up.

Following, for your reading pleasure, are a few exciting resources:

Military Spouse Corporate Career Network (MSCCN) (www.msccn.org): This program "specializes in vocational training, volunteer and employment workshops, and job search seminars at no cost to military installations and military-affiliated applicants." It is dedicated to providing career opportunities and job portability for military spouses. The best part is it was created and is operated by military spouses.

Military Spouse JobSearch (www.militaryspousejobsearch. org): This website is designed for military spouses. There is a "New Jobs" meter on the website so you can see the latest jobs available.

Military Spouse Career Advancement Account program: This is a new program I feel will make a huge difference for military spouses. Recently implemented by the Department of Defense, this program provides resources and funds (several thousands of dollars) for spouses' education in portable careers. This program may be accessed through Military OneSource (www.militaryonesource.com). Some portable careers are:

★ Education

★ Health care

★ Designing websites, newsletters, etc.

★ Medical transcribing

★ Human resources

★ Working on hardware, software, and engineering projects

★ Financial services

★ Homeland security

★ Construction

★ Cooks, chefs, bakers

★ Hospitality planners

Other portable careers include network marketing/direct sales types of businesses. In the right economy, these can provide a flexible and rewarding choice. Some network marketers are:

★ Nu Skin

★ Amway

★ Mary Kay

★ Avon

★ Pampered Chef

Take the time to do research. When researching these businesses, look for growth and innovative products that people want. One way of checking for growth is to look at the company's stock market history. Also, talk to others who have been successful with these businesses.

Whether you like books, websites, or networking, a good job is available for you. Make up your mind that you can have a rewarding career as a military spouse. Many have paved the way for us and offer their guidance. Start dreaming and get ready to step forward to the exciting world of possibilities!

Obstacles don't have to stop you. If you run into a wall,
don't turn around and give up. Figure out how to climb it,
go through it, or work around it.

—**Michael Jordan**

Nickie loses clients

Nickie, a hair dresser told me, "I lose all my faithful
clients every time we move, and it takes forever to gain
new ones. About the time I have a steady income and
clients, we move again."

THE GUILT OF LEAVING YOUR CHILDREN

Any working parent has experienced the guilt of leaving a child
at a day care, being unable to see the school play, or missing a
little league game because of his or her work schedule. The
main difference between these common concerns and those of a
long-distance military couple is the spouse who stays home has
even less time to attend these functions because he or she is acting as a single parent. When your service member is home and
you have to work during one of these school functions or little
league games, he or she can often give your child the support by
attending these important events.

I used to feel bad when I had to work weekends while my
husband was on deployment. Our son would spend long days
and nights at the sitter's while I worked. My son was in school at
the time, so my days off during the week never seemed to make
up for the lost time over the weekends. But when my husband
was home and I worked on weekends, my son had someone to
be with, and the guilt of leaving him wasn't as strong. Those days
gave them a chance to be together without Mom around.

Judy told me, "I currently have a job, but I'm going back to
my old career—raising my children!" Ella said she is taking this

year off to spend time with her family. I admire these women for deciding to stay home. Their husbands love the extra attention, and their families seem happier.

Many of the retired service members I've worked with in the past have told me that they wish they'd spent more time at home during their military careers. No one wishes he or she had spent more time at work. Many have realized now that it's too late and that their children needed them at home. They come to blame themselves for a teen or young adult who's out of control or unhappy.

Many spouses want to spend more time at home with their children. I'm not saying all spouses should be stay-at-home moms, but I'm only illustrating that many spouses find that being at home with their children and working a part-time job or just being at home is the best of both worlds, especially during deployments.

Barbara's decision not to feel guilty

"I thought at one time that I would feel guiltier for not working. When my youngest was born, though, I did not even feel a bit guilty for not going back to work. I've been home with my kids for six years now, and I think it would make me feel guilty if I wasn't home when they got back from school. I couldn't bear to tell them that they couldn't be involved in an activity because of my work schedule."

Each family is unique, and each has its own needs and wants. Some spouses who are fortunate enough to stay home, don't do well being around their kids all day. Marcie told me, "All I do is yell. I feel like my mother, and that's the last thing I want for my kids. When I was working, I seemed to have more patience." Some spouses long to be home with their kids, but financially they can't do it. As well, many military spouses can stay home and enjoy being there. They love raising the children, participating and volunteering in school-related functions, and keeping the house in order. On the other hand, many love to work. If they plan ahead, do their research, and network, they can do home-based projects or work out of the house in some capacity while taking care of the children and home at the same time quite successfully. We all know what our limits are, what we can and cannot do, and what will work for the family and us. You're the only one who knows what's best for your family.

★　★　★

TIPS TO REMEMBER

1. The most important job we will ever have is raising our children.

2. Many retired service members wish they had attempted to spend more time at home during their military career.

3. Sick leave from work will have to be used to take care of your children's medical needs, as well as your own.

4. The hours of most day care centers may limit your finding a job where you do not work past 5:30 P.M.

5. The frequent moves required of a military couple make building a traditional career difficult for any spouse of a service member.

6. Some careers will transfer from state to state, but your pay may start at the bottom again.

7. Federal employment or home-based businesses are a great career choice for military spouses.

8. Resources, programs, and books geared for military spouses are available. Research, research, research.

9. You should never give up on your dreams.

Chapter 7

HOME FRIES

FAVORITE HOME FRIES/RESOURCES

ALL MILITARY HOUSEHOLDS NEED a few "military-specific" staples to have on hand, especially during deployments. The following is not an all-inclusive list, but some of the main "meat and potatoes" that will help you endure even the longest of deployments. New programs, websites, books, and so forth are emerging all the time, so be proactive in your research to find the ones that best suit your and your family's needs.

Must-have websites

www.militaryonesource.com: This is your catchall website. I have its toll-free number stored in my cell phone (1-800-342-9647). There are operators standing by 24/7/365. The operators are master's-level consultants and offer everything from child care, counseling, relocations, job links, scholarship info, to anything and everything you may need. It's a service we all need to take full advantage of, and best of all, it's *free*.

www.nmfa.org: National Military Family Association (NMFA), "The Voice for Military Families," is an organization for all uniformed services. It is a huge advocate for improving our quality of life. It offers too many services to list. This is another website you need to have in your "bookmarks/favorites." NMFA sponsors Operation Purple camps for children of deployed service members.

www.military.com: "We started Military.com in 1999 to revolutionize the way the 30 million Americans with military affinity stay connected and informed. Today, we're the largest military and veteran membership organization—10 million members strong. Connects service members, military families and veterans to all the benefits of service—government benefits, scholarships, discounts, lifelong friends, mentors, great stories of military life or missions, and much more."

www.militaryhomefront.dod.mil: This is the Department of Defense website for "official Military Community and Family Policy (MC&FP) program information, policy and guidance designed to help troops and their families, leaders, and service providers." Whether you live the military lifestyle or support those who do, you'll find what you need. One of the great resources on this website is "Plan My Move." Moving is just part of the military lifestyle. All the information you need to plan a successful move is on this website.

www.cinchouse.com: CinCHouse, pronounced "sink-house," which represents the "Commanders in Chief of the House," was founded by Navy wife Meredith Leyva and author of *Married to the Military*. "CinCHouse's mission is to provide information, resources, and a community of friends to help you survive the toughest times and enjoy the adventures of military life."

Talk radio via Internet: For all military spouses

www.armywifenetwork.com (don't let the name fool you): This is your virtual support group 24/7/365. The blogs alone will keep you sane during deployments and your late-night insomnia sessions. It's for *all* military spouses. You won't be sorry for getting involved in this Web-based empowering, fun, interactive, "live" support group! "Army Wife Network is the internet's leading website for Army wives, by Army wives."

"Some call her the Oprah of the Armed Forces."
—**Katie Couric,** about *Army Wife Talk Radio* (previous name)

"It's a lifeline for loved ones left behind."
—**Shepard Smith**, about *Army Wife Talk Radio*

www.mymilitarylife.com (this used to be *Navy Wife Radio*): "Meet. Share. Chat. A social network for military spouses. Find a friend & Join the conversation."

Magazines

www.milspouse.com (*Military Spouse,* by military for military): This monthly magazine is always full of up-to-date info on military spouse life. A year subscription makes an awesome gift!

www.militarymoney.com (Military Money): "Explore such personal finance issues as money management, home and family life for military families, education and career advice, deployment and relocation, and transitioning to the civilian world."

Newspaper

www.militarytimes.com: *Military Times* offers all the latest information for service members, spouses, and families about pay, health, finances, and so on. It specializes with each branch having its own version (*Air Force Times, Army Times, Marine Corps Times,* and *Navy Times*). I feel this weekly newspaper offers a wealth of knowledge for our military families. A year subscription would make a wonderful gift for any service member.

Books by military spouses, for military spouses

There are too many to list here, but please take the time and go to Amazon.com, Barnesandnoble.com, or your favorite bookstore and type in *"military spouse books."* You can read the reviews and then check back to see if Military OneSource offers your choice in its library for free. If not, many sites offer free shipping for orders over a certain amount. Stock up!

Also, many exchanges are starting to carry military spouse books and magazines. If you would like to see these types of books in your local exchange, let the manager know. They aim to serve the best customers in the world!

Join a vision that one day all military exchanges will have a resource section and carry many of the wonderful books and magazines by military spouses for military spouses.

Educating and empowering yourself through books, websites, talk radio, and attending support meetings or activities offered on your installation will only enhance your life as a military spouse. I cannot encourage you enough to get involved with military life and surround yourself with military spouses. It's often the ones who are never involved or refuse to "marry into the military lifestyle" who suffer the most, who complain the most, and who have the longest and loneliest deployments and relationship problems. If you have a neighbor or know of other spouses who are being hermit crabs, reach out to her or him and invite that person to attend events. Sometimes all someone needs is an invitation or an offer to ride along. Not all of us are social butterflies. We are here to help each other bloom.

THANK GOODNESS FOR . . .

TiVo/Digital Video Recorders/On-Demand

I never thought I would succumb to these but . . . deployments have a way of causing us to rethink. Number one, we all know or will find out, during deployments our life can turn upside down/inside out. We will have to miss our favorite TV shows due to meetings, extra parenting responsibilities, more social outings (for the sake of sanity), and so on. Having the DVR (digital video recorder) technology to have all our favorite shows recorded and at our fingertips 24/7 can seem like a lifesaver. Especially during those days and mostly nights that never seem to end or become extremely lonesome. We can get lost and become absorbed with all our favorite shows just when we may need a mental break from reality. It's a great way to get through some of our challenging times. Second, my husband has a few special shows he enjoys and had to deploy shortly after the season started. I was able to have them all recorded and ready for his return, and we enjoyed watching them together while we ate dinner on our TV trays on weekend nights. Talk about a cheap date!

If your budget doesn't allow this extra expense, it may be worth hinting to your family that it would be a desired Christmas or birthday gift. Another option for watching TV shows or movies is to visit www.hulu.com. It is a free website that has a large selection to view on the computer.

TV dinners

Have you ever noticed how your eating habits change when your loved one is away? How we amazingly have an appetite for big home-cooked meals when someone is around to enjoy them, but the minute they leave, we are off to the fast food, the drive-through, or the freezer section. Some of our waistlines may shrink or suffer during this time. Our children don't seem to mind this treat; most kids would love to have pizza rolls every night for dinner if it was up to them.

Of course, you know that depending on the length of your service member's deployment this type of eating should be limited to a week or so after the departure. Too many long-term health-related problems, budget drains, interference with the routines in place will come from this type of lifestyle. The fast-food treats can be enjoyed once a week or every other week. They can be used for an emergency meal or fun times so that they do not lose their novelty. Many of my suggestions may seem obvious, but repeating them may make you think twice about going out or ordering in. A number of recipes that include quick, inexpensive, and healthy main meals are available on the Internet.

Marissa's story

"I enjoy getting a break from cooking big meals all the time, but on the other hand, I feel something is missing from dinnertime. I try to make up for the simple meals with at least one pot of vegetable soup or homemade chicken noodle soup, with veggies added, at least once a week. This makes me feel like we have a nutritional meal at some point and our bodies won't suffer too much."

Having a sit-down family dinner is a good family meeting time, and I know kids enjoy having their parent's attention.

Tommy and dinner TV

Tommy, a teenage boy I was interviewing told me, "I wish my parents wouldn't watch TV during dinner so that we can have time to have family conversations."

I know many of us eat dinner with the TV on, not realizing we are missing precious time we can spend in quality conversation with our kids. I wondered how many other children, or families crave the attention that is given to the TV.

Vehicle maintenance

Many of our service members are talented enough to maintain their own vehicles when they're home. Don't forget to add the extra expense for vehicle maintenance while your service member is on an extended deployment somewhere. We've all heard that mechanics sometimes take advantage of those who are less mechanically inclined. I follow the advice of Trish: "The more you educate yourself, the less you can be taken advantage of."

It bothers me when I realize how much money we save when my husband is home to do most of the vehicle maintenance, and then, while he's away, I have to pay someone twice as much. I wish I had taken those extra expenses into account while he was deployed on long tours. I thought about taking one of those mechanic courses so that I could change my own oil, but that thought never materialized. If you're like me, you don't like to get dirty or greasy.

One male spouse told me he was asked to give classes to his Family Readiness Group. If you have male spouses in your group, by all means, pick their brains and talents to benefit the group. I believe we all have something to offer.

Lori and Paula share mechanic stories

Lori advises, "My husband finds me a trustworthy mechanic, so when he is gone, I feel comfortable taking my car to him without my husband present. I feel like I'm less likely to be taken advantage of. I never acknowledge that I'm home alone though."

> Paula told me, "I think many repairmen take advantage of women. That's why I take someone with me who knows more about mechanics than I do. I only authorize repairs that I came for. The shop has to call me first about anything else and give me time to check it out with a knowledgeable friend."

Warranties

I think everyone, not just military couples, should try to purchase appliances with warranties.

> ### *How Beth buys appliances*
>
> "I buy all my appliances and yard tools from Sears because of the extended warranties. I can't afford to have them fixed every time they break down, and they will break down. I like how Sears will send a technician to my home. I'm not able to load up the riding lawn mower and take it someplace to be fixed."

She is absolutely correct. I was sold on the idea. I can't load up the lawn mower either, so from now on—it's Craftsman from Sears with an extended warranty. Of course, there are other great brands and services out there.

Facebook/MySpace . . .

Some of the websites that unit spouses are using—chat rooms, family support sites, and self-help sites—are a great source of information if they follow COMSEC and OPSEC procedures. There seem to be a few sites in direct violation of security procedures. This problem needs to be fixed quickly. It's not good practice to offer information about you personally—names, ages of your children, home or work addresses, or rank of your service member. Remember what we discussed in chapter 2 about personal security. I can't stress this enough. If you have questions as to whether information on a unit website may be sensitive, ask someone in a leadership position and have it checked out.

Friends

Have you noticed how often we depend on friends when our loved ones are away? Karla told me, "I need to communicate with someone over three feet tall." I can't say enough about finding a true friend. Those of us who move from place to place must become proactive. I know some of you are quiet and shy and not socially aggressive. You must make yourself available to meet others and not pass up opportunities when they arrive. You never know who can become a new best friend. Attend unit functions and other social gatherings even if you don't feel like it. You might be surprised and meet someone you enjoy hanging out with!

Iris's story

"I was walking in my new neighborhood one day, shortly after we moved in, and I noticed a lady sitting on her front porch. We both waved, and my first instinct was to keep on walking, but something told me to stop and introduce myself. She was very friendly and told me how she would have stopped by my house sooner to welcome me to the neighborhood, but she had just had back surgery and could hardly walk. I was so thankful I took the time to meet her. This gave me a nice feeling about my new neighborhood too."

Remember, you're the new person and most people have a daily routine. Making the effort to meet others is just as much your responsibility as for them to meet you. In the past, it seemed to take so long to get together with people, and when I finally did, it was time to move again. I've since made a commitment not to wait for others to ask my family over to dinner, but to be the one asking others to join us. If we don't click, then no harm's done. But if we do, then what a reward! Some couples who often move tend to keep to themselves. When you allow yourself to become withdrawn, you are cheating your families out of the best times life has to offer.

Sam's view of friends

"I think we don't take time out of our busy schedules to be thankful for true friendship. Having friends keeps the loneliness away."

★ ★ ★

TIPS TO REMEMBER

1. Take pride in keeping the home front strong.
2. Make friends because we depend on them when our loved ones are away.
3. Do not offer personal information in chat rooms.
4. Watch how your eating habits change when your loved one is away.
5. Pay attention to your kids at dinnertime. Turn off the TV.
6. Authorize only the repairs that you discussed with a mechanic before leaving your vehicle.

7. Purchase appliances with warranties.

8. Discover the empowering websites and books by military spouses for military spouses.

9. Consider having TiVo/DVR. It's a great escape.

Chapter 8

HOMECOMING

AT LAST YOU'VE MADE IT through another deployment and are looking forward to the return of your loved one, with both excitement and sometimes apprehension. You can't wait for things to get back to normal, but many of you know from experience that it takes time to readjust to family life.

FIRST NIGHT

You find yourself getting anxious and planning how you want the homecoming to be. You may have plan A, and of course backup plan B, but it's often unplanned C that takes place. You worry about those extra pounds gained or the hair color that didn't turn out quite right or the overspending you must explain, but you tell yourself that the sexy new outfit will be just right for your first night together, or will it?

Lina's sexy story

"I was dressed in a very sexy outfit when my husband returned from his last deployment, and the first words out of his mouth were 'You look like a streetwalker.' I was crushed, and the rest of our evening was not what I'd planned."

You know what taste your service member has, and you should take that into consideration when planning your homecoming reunion. If your loved one doesn't like you to wear sexy clothing in public, now is not the time to dig out the fishnet stockings. If he likes that type of clothing, but is a jealous man, wait till you are at home to dress that way.

Some clothes hide extra pounds more than others do. If that's an issue, don't wear skintight pants that are going to draw attention to your weight. I can't believe I've written this much on clothing, but so many women have told me these stories, I feel it's only fair to pass them on.

Unplanned C

The first night can be a surprise. You've planned and thought about this moment for so long, and now you find you may have consumed too much wine, you feel exhausted because of the extra cleaning, or friends and family have stopped by to welcome your loved one home so that you have stayed up way past your normal bedtime. Unplanned C has just been enacted.

Take precautions if you don't want to be interrupted. If you're up early on homecoming day, take a nap so that later you won't feel worn out. Replace wine with your favorite nonalcoholic drink. The kids will be just as excited as you will be, and they will not want to go to bed at their regular time. Those of us who have been through this have learned from past experience—couples need to know that the homecoming can be just as stressful as the departure day.

Homecoming for Tonya

"About a week before our unit was to return from an extended deployment, I was attending a unit function conducted by the chaplain, and the topic was, Homecoming. The spouses heard a lot of good information, and just before the meeting ended, the chaplain stated: 'Now, ladies, remember, when your husbands return, they're not going to be a Crock-Pot the first few nights, but more like a microwave.' All the ladies about fell off their chairs and laughed all the way home."

Tonya told me she has never forgotten that saying; I won't either. I feel it's worth passing on to you.

Wilma told me, "My husband has to date me all over again. I can't get into the intimate part of our relationship until after a few days of getting to know each other." Needless to say, their homecomings have additional stress. We all have to give and take in a relationship, especially a military marriage. Sometimes one will have to give more than the other does, but in the end, it usually works out.

April told me, "I think we all prepare differently. I always want to look my best when he is due home. Not necessarily a new outfit, but something that I know he likes to see me in. I usually arrange for someone to keep the kids overnight a couple of days after he gets home. I would feel guilty sending them away the first couple of days."

Again I ask you, how many of your civilian friends can say they've had more than one honeymoon per marriage? Most will look at you with envy when you tell them you've had dozens of mini honeymoons. Every time your loved one comes home from an extended trip, you share this experience. Some of the honeymoons can last months, but usually a week or two is the norm.

Yolanda, Susan, and Wanda and their harmonious honeymoons

Yolanda told me, "The honeymoon lasts till he makes me mad." Susan told me, "It varies—sometimes five minutes, sometimes five days, and sometimes five weeks!" My friend Wanda writes, "We are still on our honeymoon, and it's been thirty-eight years now!"

When my co-workers would ask me how I could be married to a military person who is always away, I tell them that it keeps our relationship strong and that we learn to appreciate each other. I have witnessed many couples who take each other for granted. I wish they knew how much they really loved each other. I feel that long distance often opens your eyes to what you have and how much you miss it. We've all heard the saying, "You don't know what you've got, till it's gone."

READJUSTMENT

Just like the first few weeks after deployment, the readjustment I talked about in chapter 1 starts all over again with the homecoming. What was considered normal before deployment has changed now, and new routines have been established. Both partners need to understand this. It takes time to shift back into a family routine.

For the service member, now is a good time to relax and observe the household functions without being critical or wanting to change everything that's different from before he or she departed. Realize the family has survived without you, and what works for them during deployments will be different from what works when you're home.

For the spouse, I know you can't wait to give some of those added responsibilities you inherited back to your loved one, but this does not have to happen the day after he or she returns, especially from a combat deployment. Allow service members time to relax and get their minds back into normal life again. Gradually, both partners will fall into their roles within the family. I'm sure your loved one will request some favorite dishes, so it's time to start cooking full meals again. This adjustment could make you feel resentful.

> Many of us don't look forward to the extra laundry or the extra things lying around the house. Don't think your loved one can't pick up on resentful vibes.
>
> When these types of thoughts enter your mind, replace them with all the good thoughts of having your loved one back—my grass cutter is home, my mechanic is home, my child's father and babysitter is home, my lover and best friend is home!

The homecoming can be stressful for the children when the service member returning is the disciplinarian of the family. If you find yourself allowing this to happen, you are setting yourself up for hardship. If you do not share the responsibility for administering discipline, and you have told your children things such as "Just wait till your father gets home" or "Wait till your mother hears about this," and so on, the child may fear Mom's or Dad's return.

This time will also be an adjustment for the family member, usually moms, who has conducted most of the discipline while her spouse was away. The one returning may not want to discipline the children because of being away for so long. That's no reason to let the kids become wild just because Mom or Dad has returned. Both partners should talk about and agree on discipline. Children shouldn't fear Dad returning home, even when discipline is necessary.

Nancy told me she grew up with a military father and hated when he came home from deployments. He would physically discipline her sister and her, which their mother never did while her dad was away. Nancy told me her mother would often say to her sister and her, "I'm going to tell your dad," and that would scare them. Many of us have probably said the same thing, but it often conveys to the child that Dad is the bad guy, and Mom is incapable of being in control unless Dad is there.

ACCOUNTING FOR MONEY SPENT

When your spouses are on deployment, they usually receive extra pay. When they come home, they will want to know where all the money is. You're left to explain, and all of a sudden you find yourself getting defensive. Keeping track of unexpected expenses while your loved one is away will help you remember. These expenses add up and are easy to lose track of.

Extra expenses during deployments:

* ★ Vehicle maintenance
* ★ Replacement of money spent prior to deployment
* ★ Extra food money: fast food, prepackaged, and so on.
* ★ Extra day care and babysitting fees
* ★ Care packages
* ★ Extra entertainment

Shawn told me, "I was accused of overspending, and all I did was survive." This can cause hard feelings and more stress.

My friend Ariana told me, "As long as his commander or finance companies aren't after him, he never wants to know about the money."

I used to feel like I overspent when my husband went away, but after I started keeping track of the unexpected expenses, I quickly realized where the extra money had gone and could better explain that to my husband.

Keep in mind, the one who is away will often buy little gifts the week or two prior to returning home.

Giny's comments on gifts

My friend Giny told me her husband had spent hundreds of dollars on gifts the week prior to his return from Korea. He bought Korean silk blankets for her and his family. All the while, she had been eyeing a new comforter set for their bedroom for months. She hadn't bought it yet because she didn't want to ruin the budget. Then her husband shows up with silk blankets that she didn't fall in love with and couldn't return. She was frustrated to say the least. These types of things need to be discussed before they ruin a long-awaited homecoming.

THE APPRECIATION QUESTION

Several military spouses have told me they don't feel their service member appreciates all they do and endure during deployments. Some couples have a hard time showing, or communicating, their appreciation, leaving one or both partners feeling taken for granted. We are so caught up feeling sorry for ourselves or frustrated with all we must do that we forget what the other has had to endure.

For example, one service member wrote a letter about spending Christmas holiday patrolling minefields, and then spending his daughter's birthday stopping a madman from achieving wicked and immoral goals. The next time the service member calls home and his wife complains about something trivial, he will feel unappreciated and out of touch.

If we fail to show our appreciation to our loved one, it may be hard for him or her to show any appreciation in return. Being grateful is difficult at times especially when we must remain behind to deal with all the daily activities, but we have to remember, we are in the relationship together and it takes two. One of us will have to give more than the other does occasionally. This imbalance may seem harder on you at times; however, other times we find our loved one faced with a life-or-death situation during a deployment, and we tend to forget about who is sacrificing more. We pray he or she comes home alive. The key is not to be afraid to be the first one to let the other know how much you appreciate what your partner has endured during your time apart!

Have you ever noticed that after the homecoming all those long thought-out discussions you wanted to have never happen? Things we dwelled on while our loved one was away don't seem as important after the return. Warning: These thoughts will surface again on the next trip or deployment. Write the thoughts down you feel are important and talk about them before the next trip. Otherwise, you'll want to kick yourself for not getting things cleared up while you had the chance. On the other hand, remember what we talked about earlier and "the power of thoughts." Now is a good time to reflect on some of the negative thoughts you had while you were apart. Recognize how you let them get out of hand, and realize the need to control them. Now that your loved one is in your arms, talk away.

Paul, a close friend at work, told me he couldn't help but think his girlfriend was cheating on him every time they spent time apart. He told me she had never given him a reason to think these things, but he thought them anyway. He was tormenting himself, and whether he thought so or not, I'm sure he passed on the vibes to his girlfriend. Stand by the commitment that you will trust each other until proven otherwise.

When the homecoming becomes nothing more than another day, another argument, or another mouth to feed, then it's time to look at your long-term goals and ask yourself if this is how you want to live your life. I'm all for commitment and lasting relationships, but if you cannot, or refuse to grow in your love, health, and happiness together, then it may be time to change and move on.

★ ★ ★

TIPS TO REMEMBER

1. Readjustment is not a fast process. It takes time.
2. The first night you are home with your loved one may take you by surprise.
3. Both you and your partner need to show and tell how much you appreciate each other.
4. Distance often makes you aware of how much you love your partner and how much you take for granted when he or she is around. Enjoy the honeymoon!
5. Your service member should not be expected to take back his or her responsibilities the first day or week home. Give him or her a little time to unwind.

6. Both parents should be a part of the discipline process.

7. Your spouse may want to know where all your savings are and to see a full accounting of expenditures, so make sure you have discussed your financial plans ahead of time.

Chapter 9

WOUNDED WARRIORS =
WOUNDED FAMILIES

SOME OF US HAVE NEVER THOUGHT much about our service member being wounded. We spend so much time focusing on the thought of him or her possibly not coming home. We tend to think of the worst-case scenario; it's natural. We need to spend a few pages discussing "wounded warrior" issues (seen or unseen). This could be an entire book in itself, but my goal here is to heighten your awareness to the possibility of your service member becoming wounded (seen or unseen).

> One thing you need to know up front, when anyone in the family is wounded, the entire family becomes wounded in one way or another.

My husband and I spent five months at Walter Reed Army Medical Center after he was diagnosed with a brain tumor. Our time and experience there opened our eyes to how poorly prepared most of us are in dealing with an ill or wounded family member. It can and often will be total chaos! I do not write this to scare you. You must take time to make a few plans "just in case" this should happen in your family. As hard as it will be, if you do a few things now, you will be somewhat prepared and not completely lose your mind!

SI/VSI

What in the world does SI/VSI mean? "Seriously injured" or "very seriously injured." Most of us have never heard these terms before and don't have a clue what they mean. These are the terms you will hear over the phone should your service member become injured in combat. (The only time someone should ever come to your door in military dress uniform is to notify you of a death of your service member, not of an injury, or that he or she is missing in action.) The way the system is supposed to work is: You or whoever the service member has listed as "next of kin" will receive a phone call from the Department of Defense telling you that your service member has been SI (seriously injured) or VSI (very seriously injured). At that time the Department of Defense may or may not have much information to share with you other than your service member is being transported to a medical facility (such as Germany or Stateside). You will be given a contact number and left to wait for further instructions. The "rear" command group will also be notified and should be in contact with you to help you navigate what/when/how you will proceed from this point.

It's important to note that you should *never* give personal information over the phone until you know for certain whom you are talking with. At one installation, spouses were being called and told their service member was injured and the caller was seeking private and personal information. Should you ever receive a call seeking this type of information immediately notify your command group.

Now if this isn't enough to make your head swim, it's only just begun. . . .

You have just received a phone call telling you your service member has been SI. What now? That's what every spouse/family member asks himself or herself and most often the answer is "Help!" Having witnessed firsthand the brave actions of so many family members who either packed up their vehicles or took the first flight to join their wounded service member at his or her bedside was a life-changing experience. I heard story after story of how they never thought this would happen or how overwhelming it is to see your service member wounded.

You need to spend some time and think about what you would need to take with you for an extended period should you need to be by your wounded service member. First, know you will have lots of help.

Here are some things you can do:

- *Have a plan for who will keep your kids, especially if they are in school, and/or your pets.* Whether it's grandparents, family members, or friends, think about leaving your kids for an extended period of time. I know this sounds harsh, but if you have to deal with a VSI loved one, whose life is hanging in the balance, you will not and cannot leave his or her side. When my husband was recovering in intensive care, the last thing on my mind was leaving his side. I've seen seriously wounded service members and their brave spouses staying by their hospital beds, not knowing if their service member would make it through the night or week, or how many surgeries lay ahead, so trust me . . . you will not be able to leave. Your days will run together and you will eat, breathe, and sleep medical terms, procedures, fears, decisions, and so on. As difficult as it may sound, taking the kids to Walter Reed or other military facilities treating wounded warriors is not a good idea—at least not at first. You will see injuries like you can't imagine. You will be mentally and physically exhausted dealing with the needs of your service member and trying to find time to eat and take care of yourself, let alone your children. Of course, this all depends on the extent of his or her injuries.

- *Have a plan for how you will pay your bills.* This includes things like having a "bill book" where you record your bills each month and have your passwords and websites/phone numbers written down in a safe place. You can take your "bill book" with you and conduct your business from the medical facility. Most all facilities will have everything you will need and lots of help to assist you once you arrive (computers, Internet, phone cards, and so on).

- *Have a plan for overseas travel.* If your service member is too injured to be transported to the States, you will want to go to Germany and be with him or her. Do you and the kids (if you decide to take them) have passports? The military will make arrangements to get you one if needed, but this could delay your travels by several days. Think about it . . . do you want to be delayed one minute? Passports are not cheap, but something to ponder.

- *Have an emergency fund.* No matter what, we all need an emergency fund. For the most part, the military will try to meet all your needs, but it will often take time for reimbursements to take place, so it's always good to have funds readily available for things like hotels and food.

These are only a few basic things you can do now to prepare yourself in case your service member is wounded and hospitalized. Having a basic plan will come in handy if needed. Things will fall into place and you will have people around you to help you, but your children, pets, and bills are things you have control over and a little planning ahead will pay big dividends if ever needed.

POST-TRAUMATIC STRESS DISORDER

If you're like me, the words "Post-Traumatic Stress" were something I related to the Vietnam era or a victim of a horrific crime. With the war on terrorism, all that has changed. If you're a military spouse and your service member has been deployed to combat, I'm sure you know of someone, have heard of someone, or personally experienced your loved one suffering a form of stress disorder. The last thing most service members would consider admitting to is having Post-Traumatic Stress Disorder (PTSD). Many fear it will have negative consequences on their careers as well as society in general.

A PTSD Story

If your service member is like mine, even if he felt he might have symptoms of PTSD, the possibility he would ever seek treatment is very unlikely. We are dealing with warrior mentality, and PTSD is not in their vocabulary. I personally know several spouses who have shared their concerns about their service member experiencing high levels of stress. I want anyone reading this to know, you are not alone, and there are several agencies in place where you may find help. If not for your spouse, then for you and for a way to deal with the signs and symptoms of PTSD.

Discussing and admitting to PTSD

I've been reassured that our service members are receiving training and checkups dealing with PTSD. I think that's great; however, some service members I've discussed this with have told me they won't tell the truth during these question-and-answer-type sessions. Again, the fear of hindering their career outweighs seeking help for what many feel they can handle on their own.

One way to solve this problem—require regular PTSD training in a group meeting, where everyone, not just those who have asked for help, receives specific information on how to deal with issues related to combat stress. The more PTSD can be discussed in a group setting, and not have a service member feel like he or she is being pointed out, the more participation will probably occur overall. Service members may attend such meetings and not say a word, but you can bet they are listening to everything being said, especially if they feel that the information may pertain to them. Group meetings may be the only way some service members will ever receive help.

> Military spouses also need training and education in PTSD: how to identify it, ways to help, and when to seek professional help. We are the ones who have to live with a husband or wife day in, day out. Spouses should receive training similar to that of service members.

In my own unofficial investigation, many spouses are finding themselves dealing with a loved one who is suffering from combat-related stress and have no understanding or training on the subject. I'm not knocking our great military as a whole and I know they are putting programs in place to deal with this issue, but until that happens at all levels, from the youngest enlisted service member's spouse to the senior spouses, I feel the information in this section can be used as a tool that may help you better understand PTSD and guide you to some other resources with expert advice.

Women and men may react differently to PTSD. Women for the most part feel that to share their feelings with others is okay, and they will discuss issues that disturb them openly. Unfortunately, our society teaches men to avoid discussing anything too personal, therefore male service members may experience symptoms of PTSD for a longer period than their female counterparts.

What is Post-Traumatic Stress Disorder (PTSD)?

According to the Department of Veterans Affairs: "PTSD may occur with some individuals following traumatic events that are generally outside the range of normal human experiences. These events may be human-made (war, airplane crash, rape, etc.) or natural (floods, hurricanes, etc.) and could easily trigger symptoms of PTSD. Symptoms may occur within hours or even up to six months or several years later."

Symptoms of PTSD include but are not limited to:

* ★ Feelings of isolation
* ★ Detachment from others
* ★ Sleep disturbances
* ★ Guilt feelings
* ★ Intrusive thoughts
* ★ Dreams/nightmares
* ★ Inappropriate behavior
* ★ Emotional conflict

According to the Department of Veterans Affairs:

★ "It is very common to have problems following exposure to war or other trauma. These stress reactions often become less frequent or distressing as time passes."

★ "Problems that result from trauma are not a sign of personal weakness."

★ "If traumatic stress reactions continue to cause problems for more than a few weeks or months, treatment can help reduce them."

What is physical activation or arousal?

This is when the body's fight-or-flight reaction to a life-threatening situation continues long after the event is over.
Common signs of "physical activation" can include:

★ Difficulty falling or staying asleep

★ Irritability, anger, and rage

★ Difficulty concentrating

★ Being constantly on the lookout for danger (hyper-vigilance)

Janet discusses husband's hypervigilance

"I think my husband experienced a time of 'hyper-vigilance' after he returned from one of his deployments. We were attending a Fourth of July show. As the crowd gathered around the lake where the fireworks were to be set off, we were standing in the front row with a great view. BAM! The first series of fireworks began, and I was somewhat shocked as I looked down and observed my husband in a squatting position on the ground next to me!

He quickly jumped to his feet and said, 'I hate that noise.' I didn't want to make a big deal about his behavior, so I acted as if ducking to the ground at the sound of fireworks was completely normal. My heart ached not only because I knew he was embarrassed but also because he seemed to be uncomfortable in the crowd. His mother was with us that night, and I think she was worried about the well-being of her son."

Coping with stress—some solutions

Many spouses have told me that after returning home from combat, their service members jump at loud noises, duck at the flash of a camera, or just seem on edge. Many veterans are irritable and have little patience. Keep in mind that this behavior is completely normal and will most likely fade with time. Awareness about PTSD on both the part of service member and spouse will help prevent hurt feelings and arguments. PTSD is not the service members' free ticket to be obnoxious when they return from a deployment, but readjustment to *normal* life takes time for service members, especially those who've been in combat.

I read an article in the *Army Times*/Lifelines section entitled "On the Edge." The article discusses how service members desire the adrenaline rush so many of them experienced daily while deployed. High intensity will often cause this. When they return home, some service members find themselves longing for the rush and may even conduct themselves in hazardous ways to achieve that same feeling. For example, driving at a high rate of speed, exhibiting daredevil-type behavior, and living on the edge.

If your service member craves this type of lifestyle, I would recommend joining Special Operations as a way to turn his or her craving into a positive and fulfilling career.

I remember all too well my days as a deputy sheriff when I would experience the adrenaline rush after receiving a hot call or notification of an emergency situation that I would need to respond to. These types of calls were the ones I especially longed for during the wee hours of the morning when I was tired. I would experience an adrenaline high for the next few hours, and my body would be in an enhanced stage of alertness. Loving that feeling myself, I can understand why so many crave it. Adrenaline is what many refer to as a natural high, and it can be addictive.

As spouses, we can help our service members and families adjust to home life by working to understand stress disorders. The more we learn, the better we will understand their behavior, especially behavior that may otherwise have confused or disturbed us. Instead of becoming angry or distancing ourselves from our loved one, we should desire to become better equipped to help them through their temporary dark time. By becoming aware of what trauma reactions are and how to cope with them, we will have a better chance of keeping our relationships balanced and filled with love and comfort. With this kind of support and understanding from his or her spouse, most service members will be able to recover faster than you think.

Please don't take PTSD and other health concerns lightly. I've touched only on some of these issues hoping you'll take the initiative to better understand PTSD and other health concerns that are relevant to military couples. This discussion has covered only mild cases, but some service members may return home with serious PTSD or other physical or mental disorders that need immediate treatment. The more you educate yourself about these issues, the more you will be able to use good judgment and know when to seek help for your service member and the rest of your family.

SUICIDE

Too often we read about another service member taking his or her own life. The military is putting new programs in place in an attempt to find a solution to the growing number of cases. Some of my friends or friends of friends have actually gone through the experience of a service member committing suicide, and it can seem like an unpredictable behavior. One girlfriend stated, "He seemed happy and I never had a clue he would do this." Another spouse whose husband committed suicide told me the same thing. With that said, what in the world can we do to help prevent suicide? Although the focus is currently on the service members who are committing suicide, there have been spouses who have committed or attempted suicide as well.

Some of the briefings I've recently attended have noted that the majority of the suicides are committed by young men and many have been attributed to relationship issues. Not to put a burden on you as a spouse or girlfriend or boyfriend, but you may want to rethink leaving or divorcing your service member during or after a deployment when he or she may not be in the best mental state. I'm not saying to stay in a failing relationship, but consider the mental state of the person with whom you're ending a relationship. The person's mental state may be the reason you are leaving. If this is the case, perhaps consider seeking professional help together to walk you through the process of ending your relationship. Who knows, you may find a way to work it out. If you suspect your service member will or has become suicidal whether you have already ended the relationship or not, don't hesitate to report it to the command group or 911.

What you can't do with somebody who has suicidal tendencies is, you can't leave them alone.—Lt. Gen. Rick Lynch

If your service member receives training on suicide prevention and PTSD, ask your command if it will offer the spouses the same training or at least a condensed version. I'm a firm believer in what's good for the service member is good for the spouse (as far as emotional and health training is concerned). If the training is not being offered, be proactive and educate yourself by finding answers to your questions and concerns. More than enough information is located on the Web and military websites that can help you better understand these unseen wounds and tragic issues.

The website for Military OneSource provides this helpful information about suicide:

Warning signs that someone you know may be seriously depressed and possibly suicidal should always be taken seriously. Without intervention and treatment, suicidal people may succeed at ending their lives.

Someone you know might be suicidal if he or she:

- Talks about committing suicide
- Has trouble eating or sleeping
- Talks about feelings of worthlessness, self-reproach, or guilt
- Exhibits drastic changes in behavior
- Withdraws from friends and/or social activities
- Loses interest in hobbies, work, school, etc.
- Takes unnecessary risks
- Seems preoccupied with death and dying
- Loses interest in their personal appearance
- Increases their use of alcohol and drugs
- Has attempted suicide before

A must website for military by military is www.notalone.com. It states:

Not Alone began with the idea of creating a space for warriors and families dealing with combat stress to come together, where they can spend time with others and start the healing process.

Not Alone is intended for:

- Warriors from any branch of service who are currently serving or have served in combat—especially those who have recently come home.
- Family members and close friends of warriors that deal with the effects of combat stress on a daily basis.
- Supporters who care about our warriors and their families.

This site offers forums, stories, and tons of resources. Be proactive and research your options.

From the little bit of training I've had and what I've read, it's most important to talk with the person you suspect is suicidal and actually come out and ask the question, "Do you plan to kill yourself?" We must never take a person who states he or she wants to end his or her life lightly.

Military OneSource states:

Never keep a plan for suicide a secret. Don't worry about ruining a friendship or relationship if you believe that someone is suicidal. Call for professional help immediately! It would be better to do something and be wrong, than to have done nothing and lose a friend to suicide.

> *Don't try to trivialize the problem or shame a person into changing his/her mind.* Trying to convince someone that their problems aren't really that bad, or that they have "everything to live for" only increases their feelings of hopelessness and guilt. If someone comes to you with thoughts of suicide, reassure them that help is available.

We all know, when any member of the family is wounded (seen or unseen), we all suffer. The family unit as a whole feels the impact of any negative behavior in or around the family. We are in this together—we are married to it, live with it, sleep with it, eat with it. Take a stand for your family and seek any help you need to protect your family from becoming permanently damaged by your service member's wounds (seen or unseen). There is no shame in being the best wife, husband, parent, or friend you can be, and sometimes that means seeking help. It's available, private, and at no cost through Military OneSource.

★ ★ ★

TIPS TO REMEMBER

1. Have a basic plan if you need to travel due to an injury of your service member.
2. Remember, most service members will not admit to having post-traumatic stress.
3. Don't take unseen wounds lightly. They can be life-threatening.
4. Ask for training on suicide prevention and PTSD. If train-

ing isn't available, be proactive and research your questions and concerns.

5. Learn to listen and be sensitive to the mental well-being of your loved one.

Chapter 10

PRAYER

WITH THE LINGERING DEPLOYMENTS, more and more of our courageous men and women are being injured, being killed, or being taken as prisoners of war (POWs). We at home may find ourselves feeling gripped with a fear of the unknown or lost in despair or overwhelmed with anxiety or all of these. As we watch the evening news, we realize any family anywhere can be faced with unexpected life-changing situations, and our hearts ache.

I have asked myself on many quiet nights during deployments, what would I do or how could I be better prepared should I ever receive news that my loved one is being held captive in some foreign country, or worse, is coming home in a coffin draped with our beautiful American flag? Even if all the paperwork is in order and worst-case scenarios have been discussed in advance, how can I mentally prepare for what no spouse, family member, lover, or friend ever wants to hear?

I believe that many of us find comfort and strength through prayer. Many of us are resilient, capable, independent spouses, but often during our darkest days we turn to the higher power we believe in to find the strength to carry on.

Most of us have rarely seen such an outpouring of love, courage, and prayer as we did after September 11. When my husband deployed shortly thereafter, my emotions were still raw from the news of such an attack on American soil. What would that mean for our military? What enemy were we now facing? How will this tragedy change us?

I remember returning home from dropping my husband off for that first deployment after September 11, having been told that the unit was unsure how long the deployment might last. I felt sick to my stomach—fear gripped me like never before. I told myself I had to be strong for our son, who was in sixth grade at the time of the attacks. I had to be strong for the other spouses in the unit who were younger and less experienced but just as terrified as I was. I remember asking myself, How am I going to make it through this? Are our lives changed forever? Will he ever come home? Will my husband be different when he returns?

I sat down in our recliner and picked up a book I'd recently started reading by Norman Vincent Peale titled *The Power of Positive Thinking*. The words seemed to jump out and speak to me in a way I can't explain. I started highlighting some of the messages that really spoke to me.

> "I can do all things through Christ which strengthen me." (Philippians 4:13)
>
> "Fill your personal and group conversations with positive, happy, optimistic, satisfying expressions."
>
> "Prayer is the greatest power available to the individual in solving his personal problems."
>
> "Who decides whether you shall be happy or unhappy? The answer—you do!"

I decided I was going to try the principles listed in *The Power of Positive Thinking* and see for myself if they really work. I've never been the same! Actually, the best decisions I make are the ones I pray about. Although I continue to seek out spiritual knowledge, I am continually amazed by the power of prayer.

Firsthand testimonies from families whose prayers have been answered are music to my ears. I find these people an inspiration. The more I search, the more I find many of their beliefs to be true and accurate. I would not have discovered many of the truths without first seeking.

The power of prayer

Many of my friends also testify to the power of prayer:

Jaime writes: "Once prayer became a part of my life, I started to hunger for spiritual knowledge. I read and studied about God and His love. My life has changed. I became a peaceful, happy, caring person. I realized there is more to life than me. I feel like we all have a purpose in life."

Paloma writes: "Do it! No matter where you are and how low you feel. Pray! As a family, as a couple, and as an individual."

John says it's hard not being in control, but he finds comfort knowing who's in control.

Sarah writes: "I am a firm believer in the power of prayer and seeking God's help in any circumstance. My belief in God is what keeps me going. He has promised never to give us any more hardships than we can bear."

Gina writes: "Prayer to me is just the ability to talk with God. He is someone who is always there, never judgmental. You can bounce ideas off Him and look for guidance in His word. He is always your friend, no matter what."

A church, temple, spouses group, or mosque community can also be a great support system for a family separated by deployment. If we spend more time educating ourselves about other religions and beliefs, we will see we have a lot more in common than we realize. I had an opportunity to spend several months with spouses from various countries. We all shared the same desires as a whole—love our children, have a happy marriage, stay healthy, and live in peace. These multinational spouses were gentle, kind, and beautiful, and we all learned a lot from each other. We are truly more alike than different.

Rossy's second family

"My church family has been a blessing to me. I have people to associate with who look at life the same way as I do. Knowing you are receiving prayers for strength and knowing I have that support has been extremely beneficial to my family and me."

Before leaving you with some of my favorite verses and quotes, I'd like to emphasize that knowledge of God and love is there for all who desire it. I have come to realize that my personal relationship with God is a comfort that I can always rely on. I have a daily relationship with God and like a close friend here on earth, I call on Him often, not only in the bad times.

Favorite verses during deployment:

- Psalm 56:3   "When I am afraid, I will trust in you."

- Isaiah 41:10   "Don't be afraid, for I am with you. Do not be dismayed, for I am your God. I will strengthen you. I will help you. I will uphold you with my victorious right hand."

- Matthew 6:27   "Who of you by worrying can add a single hour to his life?"

- Matthew 6:34 "Therefore do not worry about tomorrow, for tomorrow will worry about itself. Each day has enough trouble of its own."

- Proverbs 13:20 "The people you spend time with will influence the direction of your life."

- 2 Timothy 1:7 "God has not given us a spirit of fear and timidity, but of power, love, and self-discipline."

- Proverbs 14:1 "A wise woman builds her house, but with her own hands the foolish one tears hers down."

- Proverbs 31:10–12 "The wife of noble character who can find? She is worth far more than rubies. Her husband has full confidence in her and lacks nothing of value. She brings him good, not harm, all the days of her life."

- Proverbs 31:25–27 "She is clothed with strength and dignity; she can laugh at the days to come. She speaks with wisdom and faithful instruction on her tongue. She watches over the affairs of her household and does not eat the bread of idleness."

- 1 Peter 5:7 "Cast all your anxiety on him because he cares for you."

- Philippians 4:6–7 "Be anxious for nothing, but in everything by prayer and supplication with thanksgiving let your request be known to God. And the peace of God, which surpasses all comprehension, shall guard your hearts and your minds in Christ Jesus."

- Philippians 4:8 "Fix your thoughts on what is true and honorable and right."

- Job 23:10 "The Lord knows the way that I take, when he has tested me, I shall come forth as gold."

Favorite quotes followed by my two cents' worth in parentheses. Ponder over these and apply them to your life if possible.

"There is more hunger for love and appreciation in this world than for bread."—**Mother Teresa**

(It's so easy to be judgmental and critical. How often do we really show love and appreciation?)

"Never worry about numbers. Help one person at a time, and always start with the person nearest you."—**Mother Teresa**

(If we don't have lots of spouses show up at meetings we feel like failures)

"Enthusiasm spells the difference between mediocrity and accomplishment."—**Norman Vincent Peale**

(How many of us are enthusiastic about our volunteer roles?)

"People do not care how much you know until they know how much you care."—**John Maxwell**

(If your heart's in it, you will make a difference. Don't be shy.)

"Obstacles don't have to stop you. If you run into a wall, don't turn around and give up. Figure out how to climb it, go through it, or work around it."—**Michael Jordan**

(Don't give up—take a break if you need it.)

"The greater danger for most of us is not that our aim is too high and we miss it, but that it is too low and we reach it."
                                          —**Michelangelo**

(Always aim high and expect to reach your goals.)

"Before you agree to do anything that might add even the smallest amount of stress to your life, ask yourself: What is my truest intention? Give yourself time to let a yes resound within you. When it's right, I guarantee that your entire body will feel it."
—Oprah Winfrey

(Some of us face burnout because we don't know how to say "no.")

"Learn to say 'no' to the good so you can say 'yes' to the best."
.**—John Maxwell**

(Avoid burnout and learn to say "no.")

"Do what you can, with what you have, where you are."
—Theodore Roosevelt

(Stop wishing for bigger, better, best. Work with what you have, now.)

In honor of our multinatonal spouses, here are quotes from the Qur'an:

- Qur'an 3:104 "Let there be from among you, a group of believers who call to what is good, and will prohibit the evil."
- Qur'an 2.146 "The truth is from your Lord, therefore you should not be of the doubters."
- Qur'an 4.85 "Whoever joins himself in a good cause shall have a share of it, and whoever joins himself in an evil cause shall have a responsibility of it, and Allah controls all things."

My friend Laura requested that I include Psalm 91, which many see as a service member's psalm.

PSALM 91 (NEW LIVING TRANSLATION)

"Those who live in the shelter of the Most High will find rest in the shadow of the Almighty.

This I declare of the Lord: He alone is my refuge, my place of safety; he is my God, and I am trusting him.

For he will rescue you from every trap and protect you from the fatal plague.

He will shield you with his wings. He will shelter you with his feathers. His faithful promises are your armor and protection.

Do not be afraid of the terrors of the night, nor fear the dangers of the day,

nor dread the plague that stalks in darkness, nor the disaster that strikes at midday.

Though a thousand fall at your side, though ten thousand are dying around you, these evils will not touch you.

But you will see it with your eyes; you will see how the wicked are punished.

If you make the Lord your refuge, if you make the Most High your shelter,

no evil will conquer you; no plague will come near your dwelling.

For he orders his angels to protect you wherever you go.

They will hold you with their hands to keep you from striking your foot on a stone.

You will trample down lions and poisonous snakes; you will crush fierce lions and serpents under your feet!

The Lord says, 'I will rescue those who love me. I will protect those who trust in my name.

When they call on me, I will answer; I will be with them in trouble. I will rescue them and honor them.

I will satisfy them with a long life and give them my salvation.'"

★ ★ ★

TIPS TO REMEMBER

1. Try prayer for a week and see how you feel.

2. Remember, you can do things through God because He gives you strength. All you have to do is ask, ask, ask.

3. Understand that you decide whether to be happy or unhappy. You can control your thoughts.

4. Know that we are all God's children, and He loves each of us.

5. Remember, we have more in common than not.

6. Eliminate worrying. It is a bad habit and robs you of joy.

7. Be ready to deal with life-changing situations that occur without a moment's notice.

8. Try to dwell on things that are true, worthy, honorable, and praisewoethty.

9. Build a solid foundation and relationship with God.

10. Show more love and appreciation. We all crave it!

Chapter 11

DECISIONS WE NEVER WANT TO MAKE

I DECIDED TO ADD this chapter after the unexpected death of my close friend Christina's husband, Al, who was in the service. I can only hope that what I observed as I helped Christina through her loss can help others to be prepared to make the decisions we never want to make. I wish I didn't feel the need to include this chapter in my book. But it may be the one military couples need the most.

As a seasoned military wife, I thought I was well prepared to face the ultimate fear—the death of our loved one. My husband and I have prepared a will, and we have briefly discussed some small details if the worst should happen.

One morning I received a call from my husband telling me an ambulance had rushed our friend Al to the hospital. As I frantically dressed to meet Christina at the emergency room, I thought I could help by watching their baby while she stayed with her husband. As I walked in, service members were standing around, and one female service member was holding their baby. One of the nurses told me that Al had died. My knees felt like they were going to give out, and I was sick to my stomach. I couldn't believe what I was hearing.

The nurse told me I needed to be strong for my friend. But I was at a loss for words—I felt so weak. I couldn't imagine what she was going through, but I wanted to run to her and hold her in my arms. I felt inadequate—I couldn't do or say anything that would make her feel better. Al was young. They had just started a family, and their second child was due in just eight weeks. The disbelief was overwhelming.

When we left the hospital later, we were still in shock. I immediately called one of my best friends, Deb, a very spiritual person, and asked her to pray for Christina. I asked her to pray that I could bring comfort to Christina at this time of grief. I asked her to call two of our other friends, Laura and Elli, who I knew would pray for us too. These women are also military wives, and we have developed a close sisterhood over the years. I'm a firm believer in the power of prayer.

We returned to Christina's house, where she was then faced with decisions we never want to make. Making these decisions with her made me realize that most of us are not as prepared as we think. Several other seasoned military spouses I've talked with about the decisions required immediately following a death have told me that they too were unaware of how much there was to decide to do and how quickly it all had to happen. I knew then that I needed to add this information to my book so that others, as well as myself, would be better prepared to deal with the loss of a loved one.

None of us wants to talk about death. Al's sudden death taught me that if you or I don't take the time now to figure out exactly what to do if this situation should arise, we may find ourselves having to make decisions under emotional distress. If we don't talk with our spouse about every little detail, we may find ourselves wondering, "What would he or she have wanted?" Your grief will be hard enough to bear without the additional stress of self-doubt.

The decisions included in this chapter are usually made very soon after a loved one's passing.

Some options to consider

If your unit offers a notification form (if not, request that it does offer one), see if you have the choice of requesting to be notified only at home. The reason I say this is I know of a spouse who was at work when the notification team notified her. She later told me it was horrible. She was not in the comfort of her home, where she could go to her bedroom, fall on the floor, and cry. She told me she felt like she had to keep her composure the whole ride home, which took approximately forty minutes! She was surrounded by uniformed service members, and during the ride home, she called her brother and told him that her husband had been killed. She had no privacy.

If that wasn't bad enough, later, every time she went back to work she experienced panic attacks and could not erase the vision of the uniformed service men standing in the hall waiting to notify her that her husband had been killed. She later left her job for this very reason.

BLUF (bottom line up front): Request to have a choice and have notification forms in place at the unit so this kind of trauma does not happen to you or your friends.

Decisions We Are Required to Make

Telling the kids and family members: This is usually the first task after notification. I'm afraid this necessity is one of the hardest things anyone will ever have to do. Telling the children should take precedence over everything else.

Since the first edition of this book, I've experienced more deaths than I care to count. One thing you need to think about is if you are notified, how or when will you tell the kids? Sometimes the kids will be home when the doorbell rings. What are you going to do? Once you see the notifying service member in dress uniform and a chaplain, you already know your service member either is missing in action (MIA) or has been killed. Any other news will be told to you via telephone. Only in the event of the death of a service member or when he or she is MIA should you be notified at home. This is why it's very important to have a plan in place. Some units allow spouses to choose whom they would like to accompany a notification team by filling out a "spousal notification form." These must be local friends or family who can be present within hours of the unit being told of a death. These "chosen care team" members will support and help you until your other family members or friends arrive.

If your specific unit does not offer you choices, ask the command to change the way it conducts notification and allow spouses going through the most devastating time of their life to have a choice of who shows up at the door. The units that conduct notification in this manner have had the most success stories, and all the grieving spouses I have known who have gone through this agree it is much better to have a friend accompany a notification team than someone you may or may not know or like!

One unit that has set the standard for "notification procedures" is the Army's 160th Special Operations Aviation Regiment. Its headquarters is located in Ft. Campbell, Kentucky. Its procedures and care team training are time tested and fine-tuned. I've been told the unit shares its procedures with any unit who would be interested in following the same type of notification process. Your command group will know how to contact the unit should it choose to adopt this standard of excellence.

Suzanne, a surviving spouse, told me that getting assistance for yourself and the kids after the funeral from a counselor or psychologist is immensely valuable.

Phone log: Your house will probably be full of people—some you know well, while others may not even look familiar. The phone will continually ring as family and friends call to offer their condolences. Some calls will be from friends you haven't heard from in years.

The grieving spouse should take only important or needed calls the first few days. Ask a friend to monitor the phones and keep a log for you and take messages. Have him or her write down how the caller knows your loved one. Some callers may have known the deceased but not the spouse. You need to know exactly whom you are calling back.

People are kind, but having to talk on the phone and greet them in your home will be a huge task. Try to postpone the calls until a more convenient moment. You will need time to reflect and be alone. Don't hesitate to stop all visitors except immediate family. You can have someone outside your home to politely limit visitors.

Red Cross: Within hours of a death, you *may* receive a call from the Red Cross. At this point you will probably be in denial and shock. You will wonder what the Red Cross would need to talk with you about in these first few hours of grief.

The Red Cross will be calling to ask if you would like to donate your loved one's organs. This question may seem insensitive to you as you grieve, but keep in mind that your loved one's organs could save the life of another person's son, daughter, father, mother, and so on. Organ donation can include the heart, liver, kidneys, eyes, lung, muscle, and even bone marrow. There are many questions the Red Cross needs to ask about this process because they consider many factors when determining what organs they can harvest to help someone else.

One misconception about organ donation is that it may change the appearance of your loved one if you have an open-casket funeral. The Red Cross has stated this is not true—organ donation does not change the look of your loved one.

Even if your loved one has "organ donor" marked on his or her identification card, the Red Cross will still need your approval and a twenty to thirty-minute phone interview to record your response. The Red Cross will only have hours to harvest these organs, so your response should be determined between you and your spouse as early as possible. A twenty-to-thirty-minute phone interview is a lot to ask of a grief-stricken individual. If the decision has already been made, you will not be as upset by this untimely but necessary phone call.

Preparation: Shortly after you have been notified of your loved one's death, the military will assign a Casualty Assistance Officer (CAO). This person will walk you through tough decisions and make the necessary arrangements for you and your family. He or she will work closely with you and answer your questions.

If your loved one dies while in the United States, one of the first decisions you will have to make is which funeral home you would like to hold the wake or funeral. The military has contracts with local funeral homes, and if you choose one of these, the expenses will be covered. If you use a different funeral home, you will be given an allowance for the fees that may or may not cover all the expenses. Any cost over the allowance will be the responsibility of the surviving spouse.

From my own personal experience, as well as that of some surviving spouses, I know that if your service member dies overseas, the body will be transported back to the United States. At that time you can elect to have the body transported to the place of burial at no expense. If you decide to have the body transported to a location for a memorial or viewing but then want the body transported to a different location outside that town or city for burial, you will have to pay the difference in transportation cost. The expenses to transport the body will be covered only from point of entry to the United States to the location for burial. As with most regulations, waivers can be submitted.

This was surprising news to many spouses and families because they would have liked to have had the body transported to the local hometown or military base for memorials or viewing, and then to perhaps a national cemetery like Arlington for burial. This can be accomplished, but the families I assisted were told they would have to pay out of pocket for multi transports of the body. All of them chose to have memorials with photos and a small service at the site of burial for those who could not travel to Arlington.

You will need to decide what clothing your loved one will be buried in. Will it be a uniform? Which one? Or will it be civilian attire? Should your service member choose to be buried in a uniform, a military person will be assigned to ensure the ribbons or medals are displayed correctly.

It's best for your service member to have his or her dress uniform prepared at all times with the proper ribbons and/or medals in place. If he or she should die, there most likely will be additional ribbons or medals that will need to be added to the uniform. You will have assistance.

Will your loved one wear his or her wedding ring during viewing, and will he or she be buried with it? Some choose to have the viewing or visitation with the wedding ring on and then give it to the spouse or family member before burial.

Will you need a casket (the military furnishes both wood and metal) or will your loved one be cremated? The military provides fine caskets; Christina was guaranteed that even after fifty years, the military casket would still look the same. Should you wish to purchase a different type of casket than those provided, the military will furnish a funeral allowance, which may or may not cover the cost.

If you need to transport your loved one to a different location, out of state or country, you may still use the local funeral home contracted by the military to prepare your loved one for transportation. A military escort will travel with your loved one. The escort may be a close friend or an assigned person. Once your loved one reaches the destination you choose, he or she will be taken to a local funeral home for visitation and the service.

In order to notify the public of your service member's death, you will need either to provide information for an obituary or write one yourself. You can have a service at the funeral home, at a church or house of worship, at graveside, or at any other place you choose. The funeral director may ask if you would like to say any words, for instance, "thoughts of a loving wife or husband." The director will also ask whom you want to conduct the funeral services and whom you would like to speak at the funeral.

You and your service member should discuss if you prefer having an open (if possible) or a closed casket. By deciding beforehand, weighing out the pros and cons (such as age of the children), the in-laws and other family members won't have to be involved with that decision making. See "Suzanne's Story" later in this chapter (p. 180).

Cemetery: One of the next questions may be, Have you chosen the cemetery where you would like to bury your loved one? You'll have to choose between a local cemetery or a national cemetery.

Christina seemed to be leaning toward a cemetery in Al's hometown before she found out that it only allowed flat, inground headstones and one vase. That meant no flags on Veterans Day or Memorial Day. She was also concerned with buying an extra grave plot next to her husband so that in the future her children could bury her there. This can be an extra expense you may need to pay beyond the other fees. You are entitled to burial allowances, but these may or may not cover the price.

A national cemetery will offer the veteran and his or her spouse and children under a certain age a burial site at no extra cost. Many service members I know want to be buried in a national cemetery beside their comrades in arms.

The Veterans Administration provides two different types of headstones: upright marble or flat bronze. Depending on whether the headstone is in a national cemetery or private cemetery, you will also have to decide on the inscription placed on the headstone. The national cemeteries have a limited choice of inscriptions, whereas private cemeteries will allow you to inscribe whatever you want.

Most cemeteries have a pavilion for burial services. Once the service is complete, all people leave, and the actual "in the ground" portion takes place. You may choose to watch this interment.

Christina decided to have Al's visitation in her husband's hometown at a local funeral home and the military honors conducted at a national cemetery located approximately two hours away.

Military housing: If you live in military housing, you will have several months free of charge while you make moving arrangements. The military will pay for the cost of your move within one year of the service member's death. Rest assured, no one will kick you out of your housing right away.

Papers, papers, papers: You will also be asked to furnish original marriage licenses, any prior divorce papers for both you and your spouse, and any adoption papers. You will also need to furnish the social security cards of your children as well as your own.

Make sure these important documents are on hand. You will need to provide your insurance information if other than military insurance. The military has no choice but to provide insurance entitlements to the names listed on the service member's official military documentation. If your spouse has been married before, he or she needs to update all paperwork, including wills.

You will need to have all bills, credit cards, bank accounts, savings accounts, and car and home insurance policies changed into your name fairly quickly. For some of these accounts, you will need a copy of the death certificate, which you and your CAO will request.

The unit your service member is assigned to may want to provide the service member with some type of award. The unit will need all his or her prior awards and certificates in consideration of the new award. If you know ahead of time where you keep all these things, finding them will not be a problem.

Most units will conduct some type of memorial service, and the unit may ask you to provide several pictures of your loved one.

Entitlements: Your CAO will explain all your entitlements in detail. Entitlements often change, so I won't list them all in this book. Have a close friend or family member take detailed notes during the entitlements briefing.

Just think about making all these decisions within days after finding out your loved one has passed away. I found it overwhelming even as the friend of the grieving spouse. I've addressed the main decisions that you will need to make, but you can be sure that others will arise as the days pass.

Preparing for the worst

Take the time to fill out the simplified checklist that follows, or at least discuss the items it includes. During a time of grief, you will take comfort in knowing that you and your spouse have already answered most of the tough questions, and your grieving process will not be compounded by stress and self-doubt.

Upon notification, while sobbing, one spouse stated that her and her husband could never take the time to talk about death, that it was too painful. Now she was left to make all these decisions on her own.

Questions

The following questions will be asked of the surviving spouse within days of a death notification:

Red Cross (if applicable) within first few hours

- ★ Will you agree to donate your loved one's organs?
- ★ If yes, you will need to provide a twenty- to thirty-minute phone interview with the Red Cross worker.

Funeral details

- ★ What clothing will your loved one be buried in?
- ★ If military uniform, which one?
- ★ Will ribbons or medals be displayed on the uniform?

★ Will your loved one be buried with his or her wedding ring?

★ Do you want your loved one to have the wedding ring on during viewing and taken off before burial?

★ What type of casket will you choose, wooden or metal?

★ Will your loved one be cremated?

★ Do you have information for an obituary?

★ Where will the funeral services be conducted?

★ Would you like to say something at the funeral or have your thoughts read by someone else?

★ Would you like anyone to speak at the funeral?

★ If yes, who?

★ Will this be a military funeral?

★ Who will conduct the funeral?

Cemetery

★ Will your loved one be buried in a private cemetery or national cemetery?

★ What cemetery will your loved one be buried in?

★ If that cemetery is unavailable, give second choice, third choice. [Check to see if your cemetery of choice allows upright headstones and if veterans are honored on special occasions.]

★ For the one left behind, would you prefer a graveside funeral or pavilion service at the time of burial?

Papers

★ Do you have your original marriage license? Where?

★ Divorce papers?

★ Adoption papers?

* Insurance documents, car, home, life.
* Titles or registrations or both to vehicles, boats, motor-cycles, other recreation vehicles?
* Bills, credit cards, bank accounts, savings account.
* Service member's prior awards and certificates?
* Photos of service member and family?

Housing

* Will you be moving from your current location?
* If you live in military housing, do you know where you will move to?

Checklist—funeral arrangements

You may find this is easy to fill out and place in your lockbox or file with your important papers.

Funeral Arrangements

Organ donor

Service Member: Yes _____ No _____ any specifics: _____

    Example: Transplant only _____

Spouse: Yes _____ No _____ any specifics: _____

    Transplant only _____

Children: Yes _____ No _____ any specifics _____

    Transplant only _____

Funeral details

Address of funeral services:

Service Member: _____

      Military _____ Civilian _____

Spouse: _____

      Military _____ Civilian _____

Children: _____

      Military _____ Civilian _____

Accommodations

Service Member: Burial _____ Cremation _____ Entombment _____

                 Open casket _____ Closed casket _____

                 Wooden _____ Metal _____

Spouse: Burial _____ Cremation _____ Entombment _____

                 Open casket _____ Closed casket _____

                 Wooden _____ Metal _____

Children: Burial _____ Cremation _____ Entombment _____

                 Open casket _____ Closed casket _____

                 Wooden _____ Metal _____

Officiates

Service Member: Military chaplain _____ Civilian clergy _____

Spouse: Military chaplain _____ Civilian clergy _____

Children: Military chaplain _____ Civilian clergy _____

Clothing

Service Member:

    Uniform, which one? Or civilian clothing and what? _____

_____

    Ribbons or medals? _____

    With ring or without? Or just for the viewing? _____

Spouse:

Uniform, which one? Or civilian clothing and what? _____

Ribbons or medals? _____

With ring or without? Or just for the viewing? _____

Children:

    Uniform, which one? Or civilian clothing and what? _____

    (Scout uniform, sports uniform, favorite clothing)

    Ribbons or medals? _____

Pallbearers

Service Member: _____

_____

Spouse: _____

_____

Children: _____

_____

Cemetery

Service Member:

National cemetery:

Choice #1 _____

#2 _____

#3 _____

Civilian cemetery:

Choice #1 _____

#2 _____

#3 _____

Spouse:

National cemetery:

Choice #1 _____

#2 _____

#3 _____

Civilian cemetery:

Choice #1 _____

#2 _____

#3 _____

Children:

National cemetery:

Choice #1 _____

#2 _____

#3 _____

Civilian cemetery:

Choice #1 _____

#2 _____

#3 _____

Grave marker

Service Member:

Military (upright or flat) _____

Words or past wars: _____

Spouse:

Military (upright or flat) _____

Words or past wars: _____

Children:

Military (upright or flat) _____

Words: _____

Music

Service Member: _____

Spouse: _____

Children: _____

Special reading

Service Member: _____

Spouse: _____

Children: _____

Obituary

Service Member: _____

_____

_____

_____

_____

_____

Spouse: _____

_____

_____

_____

_____

Children: _____

_____

_____

_____

_____

Papers

Where are important papers kept? _____

★ Original marriage license? _____

★ Any divorce papers? _____

★ Social security cards for all members of the family: _____

★ Insurance: life, vehicles, home, recreation vehicles? _____

★ Titles to all vehicles: _____

★ Bills, credit card and bank information: _____

Housing

★ Where will survivors live? _____

Military spouses are often close to other spouses, and this is especially true when a death occurs. The following advice is for other military spouses who want to offer comfort to a grieving friend.

★ ★ ★

Tips to Remember for Those Who Are
Providing Comfort and Support

These words are not only from my personal observations but from surviving spouses who have offered their firsthand experiences:

1. Listen, listen, and listen. When someone is grieving or in a state of shock, he or she will need to vent. You need to listen to the person in grief. First, your friend or relatives have been turned upside down, and they may feel that life is out of their control. Second, if the support person doesn't listen to the wishes of the mourner, this can cause additional stress. For instance, if the person tells you he or she doesn't feel like going out, don't try convincing him or her otherwise. If the person tells you no about anything, take no for an answer. The person in grief may change his or her mind, and we shouldn't pressure him or her to do what we think is best.

2. Keep in mind that if you find out someone you know has passed away, the grieving family may not feel like talking with anyone but relatives and close friends. If you do not meet those criteria, wait a day or two to call and offer your condolences. My friend, Suzanne, a Gold Star Wife, the widow of a fallen service member, suggested that a sympathy card is a wonderful way to let the grieving family know you care without intruding during such a painful time. (See Suzanne's Story under Personal Account.)

3. Start a phone log immediately. The grieving person will want to know who called and will be able to choose when and whom to call back. Have the information and address of the funeral services and the address of the residence on the phone log so that anyone who is answering the phone will have access to that information.

4. Please do not show affection to your loved one in front of someone who just lost a spouse. If you and your loved one hold hands, hug each other, or show affection in any way, the one who's grieving will miss his or her spouse even more. Such behavior only reminds the one grieving of what he or she no longer has. We need to become supersensitive at a time like this. Be aware of your behavior—we often do these things without thinking.

5. Please remember, all of us have plans for the future, but when a loved one dies, you alter those plans. When someone is grieving, he or she seldom has a new plan worked out. He or she is probably thinking, "What am I going to do?" If visitors sit around discussing their future plans, this may add to the person's grief. Again, none of us does these things intentionally, but we need to be aware what we do and say in the presence of one who is grieving.

6. Take into account that once the memorial and funeral are over, the grieving family will need to get back into a routine, and this is the time when they'll need friends most. Call and offer to meet for dinner or at the library or any familiar place. Reaching out a hand in friendship and then following through is one of the nicest gifts you can give to the family. Remember to be gentle. Don't ignore what they've been through, but also don't ask a lot of questions. Let it come naturally and slowly, and make time to talk about everyday things. Helping them move on is a long and slow process.

7. Remind yourself that holidays, birthdays, anniversaries, and other significant occasions will be hard for the grieving spouse and family. On those days, make sure to call or e-mail. Stay in touch, even if it is just once a month—let them know you are thinking of them. They may have to move far away from a military installation that has become a part of their lives, and they'll need family and friends to ease the transition.

PERSONAL ACCOUNT: THE DEATH OF A SERVICE MEMBER

The following is a personal letter I received from Suzanne, a Gold Star Wife. She shares her personal experience and her advice. I hope you will benefit from her words.

Suzanne's story

"On Easter Sunday of 2004, at about 11 P.M., I was notified by two gentlemen, a chaplain and the rear detachment commander that my husband was killed in action. Once notified, I decided to call my husband's parents, family, and our older children. The two gentlemen stayed with me while I made those calls. They gave me strength to tell of his death. They called my Casualty Assistance Officer (CAO), and we set up a meeting for mid-morning the next day. Luckily, I had my dear neighbor with me as well.

"I wish I'd told my husband to put my best friend's phone number on the Casualty Notification Form that he filled out prior to deployment, because no one should be alone when he or she is told that a husband or wife has been killed. I made plans for my friend to arrive early in the morning to fend off visitors and phone calls while I broke the news to our three youngest children, who were asleep at the time of the notification. I had called our three older children the night before.

"My CAO [casualty assistance officer] arrived at 10 A.M. We talked about what he knew of my husband's death. He then outlined what his job duties were and what we were going to have to do. He told me that we would be taking baby steps not giant steps toward getting things accomplished. I was so overwhelmed.

"I didn't have the Red Cross calling because my husband was killed in Iraq, but I did have about sixty members of his unit, all the way up to the commander, visiting me that day and then the next. The Family Readiness Group (FRG) and a group of friends brought bags of groceries and started feeding people, including my kids. The FRG also arranged to bring in meals every day for a number of weeks. The process was very overwhelming. I often escaped to the privacy of my bathroom where I cried or just sat there in the quiet.

"Four days after my husband's death, the unit held a memorial service. I had provided pictures, his green beret, his boots, and a set of dog tags. By then, both sides of our family had arrived, and we were entertaining a vast number of friends and colleagues. I requested that no one stay at my home because my children needed their sleep (and I needed the peace). I was glad because it gave me a chance to have some quiet time.

"The military could not fly my husband's body out of Iraq for safety reasons, so we could not make final funeral arrangements for some time. It took over two weeks to get him to Dover, Delaware, where he had to have an autopsy. Once that was completed, a dear military friend of ours escorted his body to the national funeral home in Arlington. He also made sure that my husband's uniform was complete with awards, ribbons, and other honors. An open casket wasn't an option, we were told, due to his injuries.

"On the day of the visitation, we were allowed to view him, and the funeral home gave me one hour prior to visiting hours to spend alone with my husband. I opted to give my in-laws thirty minutes of my time so that they could say good-bye to their son.

"Open or closed casket is something that should be decided on before deployment to prevent disagreements between the spouse and other family members. I chose a closed casket visitation and funeral since my young children would be present. All of our expenses were covered under the allowance for a military funeral.

"The next day at the funeral, the Ft. Meyer Chapel was overflowing with friends, family, and colleagues. I asked both my pastor and the chaplain from my husband's unit to handle the funeral service, and they did a wonderful job. I know my husband would have been greatly honored. I chose the wood casket knowing the VA provides an American flag to drape over it.

"My husband was buried in Arlington Cemetery with full honors. We flew from Ft. Campbell, Kentucky, to Washington, D.C., for the funeral. The flight was also included in the allowance.

"Once home, the work began. You need a death certificate for many items, and obtaining one can take time. We requested a death certificate the first week after his death and received a copy almost four weeks later.

"My CAO and I also had to make sure that Tricare (Prime) and Concordia (health and dental insurance) knew of his death, and that put the children and me into a three-year span where we have certain benefits for free. After that period, we will change to retiree status and pay the retiree rate.

"We also had to handle the life insurance paperwork. Please make sure that there is an appropriate beneficiary listed. From my membership with the Gold Star Wives of America, I learned that many fallen service members didn't opt to enroll their families in Tricare or make sure servicemembers' Group Life Insurance has listed the SGLI beneficiary correctly. Many wives and children are no longer eligible for medical/dental and the SGLI because their service member didn't enroll them or confirm the beneficiary listing.

"Social Security, Veteran's Affairs, and Retirement Benefits and

Services all require a visit to each office. Take notes so you will have a record of what your benefits are.

"Short-term memory loss is common among grieving spouses. Sometimes you write something down and can't remember where you wrote it. Keeping a folder or notebook with notes is better than relying on your shocked memory. Friends have told me your memory will come back with time, and it does.

"Any bills or joint accounts need to be changed. Some may require a copy of the death certificate and some may not. Keep notes on whom you spoke with and the date and time. Also, follow-up if you are being sent information to fill out and return. The representatives you speak with don't always send the information, and you may not remember until it's too late.

"You'll have to call to report your spouse's death, which can seem surreal. The insurance company will require you to fill out some forms and to send them a certified original of the death certificate. If you have any additional insurance policies make sure that you have the money deposited into a money market account or somewhere that can earn interest until you decide exactly what to do with it. I didn't feel capable of making a good decision at the time of my husband's death, so I decided to wait.

"Most of the personal accounts and insurance details you will have to take care of yourself, so if you don't feel comfortable doing it, ask a trusted family member or friend for help. If you can, talk with a financial advisor about your future financial situation once you have an idea of what your benefits are and once you cashed in your insurance policies. Make sure to get a second opinion. Some advisors represent only certain investments, mutual funds, or banks, and so on, and may not offer what's best for you. If you don't feel comfortable doing this immediately after your loved one's death, then wait until you do.

"Remember to ask for help. Most family members and friends

are anxious to do whatever they can. Call on them. Two heads are always better than one.

"If you live on post, you will eventually have to move. This move can be difficult. Ask for help. Finding a new home, packing, moving, and unpacking are stressful. I moved off post within three months of my husband's death because seeing military families and the uniform made me very sad. I also wanted my children to start the school year in a new school rather than during the middle of the year. So I moved my family seven hundred miles away to be near my parents and sisters. I recommend moving near family members. You will find great support there.

"If you aren't organized, now is the time to improve your skills. Buy a package of folders and label them clearly. Keep them in a drawer, box, or tub where you can access the paperwork quickly and easily. Make a folder for taxes—this will save you the time and agony of searching through piles of paperwork. Make a folder for thank-yous to be written, and jot down on a slip of paper whom you need to write to and for what and then give it some time. You'll get to them eventually. Make a folder for miscellaneous receipts, that way you'll never have to worry about finding them, especially for tax purposes. Keep all your bills, accounts, death certificates in these folders in one place. You will be glad you did. Use a calendar that you see all the time to keep track of deadlines and appointments.

"Find time to take a long soak in the tub or go to a movie. Do something fun that gets you out of the house. Something as simple as going to a fast-food drive-through can be exciting.

"Find support from people who've been through the same thing. I found that chatting in the Tragedy Assistance Program for Survivors (www.taps.org) chat room was comforting. You will find other wives or mothers who've lost a loved one in the war who know what you're feeling.

"Finding help, whether from a spiritual leader, pastor, priest or a psychologist, is a good way of helping yourself cope with the grief. We all go through the grieving process differently—just focus on getting through today.

"Be patient. Give yourself time to cry, to be angry, to ask why, because these things are completely natural. Sleeplessness is also part of grieving. Talk to your doctor if you need help with anything. He or she is there to help and can be useful in this process. You know yourself better than anyone—listen to your body and take one day at a time."

★ ★ ★

TIPS FOR THOSE WHO ARE GRIEVING

1. Do not be afraid to say what you want (limited visitors, phone calls, and outings).
2. Everyone grieves differently; do not compare yourself to someone else.
3. Remember the good times, and allow yourself to laugh at the funny times.
4. Take one day at a time, and do not worry about tomorrow.
5. Do not try to plan too far in advance, things will fall into place.
6. Ask for help, and delegate tasks to family and close friends.
7. Eat and drink fluids, even in small amounts.

Did you know . . .

Most service members and spouses are not aware that if the service member has spent enough time in service (usually twenty years of active duty service) and is eligible for retirement benefits, should that service member die, upon his or her death, the surviving spouse will receive only a portion of the service member's earned retirement.

Most service members are entitled to 50 percent of their base pay upon retirement after twenty years of active duty service. If the service member dies, the surviving spouse will receive only *half* (25 percent of his or her base pay) of the service member's *earned* retirement.

The spouses I have spoken with whose husbands had served for more than twenty years were under the assumption that upon their husband's death they would receive the full retirement.

These spouses and most service members I've shared this with have been shocked to learn their family will *not* receive the full retirement should the service member die.

Chapter 12

LEADERSHIP

> If your actions inspire others to dream more, learn more, do more and become more, you are a leader.—**John Quincy Adams**

EFFECTIVE LEADERSHIP during a deployment is critical. Everyone hopes for and seeks good leadership. Currently the leadership for many of the spouses' programs/support groups is run by volunteers. Who doesn't desire and long for experienced, trained, effective, passionate, and excellent leadership? Once you've experienced it, the standard is set and that becomes the true vision of how leadership should and could be!

Many of the volunteers are going above and beyond and doing an outstanding job in making a positive difference. Unfortunately, many of these leadership positions are solely dependent on whom you are married to. I've witnessed some senior spouse leaders pour their lives into providing effective support groups while others by default are "positional leaders" who don't want the job, have not trained for the job, are not passionate about the job, and flat out don't do the job! They are pressured into filling the role because of whom they are married to, and if they had a choice, they would run as far as they could from their leadership role. Many of these spouses would love to quit, but they don't or won't! So the outcome of such a system is a support group whose effectivenesss is hit or miss depending on the leadership.

Until this system changes or is revamped we must deal with what we have. The following sections address some things you can do.

Become part of the solution and not the problem

How do you do that? I'm so glad you asked. First, no matter who the leader is, good, bad, great, or really bad, make it your mission to offer a helping hand. Offer your time, experience, talents, and assistance in everything you can. If your offer is not accepted (this is when it gets tough), keep offering. Do you realize many people feel it's a sign of weakness to accept help? If this is the case, your leader will need some time to realize you really care and accept your help.

For leaders please, please, please don't try to lead alone. This has been a huge downfall of many volunteer spouse leaders. It seems that often if the appointed leader does not have the participation of the appropriate/expected co-leader, then the leader will try to go it alone. This should never be accepted. If you search and ask personally, you will find spouses who will step up and co-lead a spousal group. Many senior spouses in leadership positions have told me no one will help them. Many other spouses have told me they would help if they were asked. So, if you are in a leadership position and are in need of a co-leader, take the time to personally ask a spouse you know or feel has the passion, time, and some experience to help you. It does not have to be the most-senior or second-senior or third-senior spouse. Take the husband's rank out of it and find someone who has the heart and time to co-lead with you. I'm not saying ignore a senior spouse, but if she or he does not have the time or desire to lead or co-lead, find someone who does. The spouses' programs need to have leadership teams. The burden is often heavy, and going it alone will likely lead to burnout and much frustration, not to mention the loneliness you will feel. Leaders need "battle buddies" too.

Don't expect your leadership members to do it all. They are volunteers and have the same difficulties during deployment as the next spouse. If you can't or won't offer your help, then keep your complaints to yourself. They do not help the team or other spouses who are coping with the challenges of deployments. Become part of the solution—join the team!

Offer to start a project

What if there is nothing going on or being planned? Call your leader and let her or him know *you* would like to spearhead whatever it is you are wanting to do (such as scrap booking, or a book club, lunch club, or walking club). In most cases, the leader will be thrilled to have some help and someone to take off some of the load. It's so hard to ask for help, but when help is offered, it's usually a welcome relief!

Show up!

Yes, you need to show up at events, meetings, anything and everything you can be present for. Just by showing up, you are showing your support for whoever is hosting the event and it's a chance to network with other spouses. You may just meet your new best friend, but you have to *show up*. Leaders cannot lead from a distance, and you can never make a difference without showing up.

Make meetings worthwhile

Leaders must do everything they can to plan their meetings and activities so that they are worth the group's time. Everything is pulling us in all directions, especially during deployments, so it's extremely important to have events that are going to be fun, informative, and worthwhile. No one has time to come out to a meeting to hear someone blah blah blah about trivial things.

Make your meetings count! One suggestion is to have everyone offer input at meetings. You could have a roundtable with each leader discussing one thing that's working well and one thing that's a challenge. This in itself will produce conversation and we are our own best teachers. Having a roundtable will solve many issues, but the leader must initiate this.

Accept that there is no "I" in "TEAM"

Stop using words like *I, me, my*. It's all about *we, us, our*. Get in the practice of thinking of your group as a team and ask for everyone's opinions and input. Give the team ownership in the group. Tell the group, "*We* are a team and *we* will make our group special." Everyone should have a say and be made to feel part of the group, especially new spouses or spouses who have never been to a group meeting. Everyone needs to go out of his or her way to welcome new spouses and embrace them into the group. We are often so busy socializing in our own little group that we never make it over to speak with the "new face."

We must get away from the "rank" issue and treat all spouses equally. I agree the senior spouse should have a place of honor, but don't place rank on it. Senior is senior whether the person is married to an officer or an enlisted service member. This is an old tradition and our new generation could care less about rank. A spouse is a spouse is a spouse (male or female). We all have the same needs and wants.

Get the word out!

What if people just don't come out no matter what you plan? It happens. One problem could be getting the word out. Don't think people are coming to your meetings with only one e-mail sent out three weeks prior to the event. It won't happen. Reminders need to be sent, and if you really want a good turnout, call people and actually ask them to come and remind them about the time and date!

Don't forget about child care

Child care is a huge issue. If on-site child care is not available, most spouses are not going to pay a babysitter for an event they are not sure is worthwhile. I recently talked to a young baby-sitter and asked her what she normally gets paid an hour for babysitting. To my surprise, she told me about $8 to $10 an hour! I know for a fact I would not pay that to attend a meeting that I didn't feel was going to be worth my time and money! Many spouses don't want to leave their children in places too far from the meetings either. Make it worth their while. We have even asked the service members to watch the children while the spouses conduct their meetings. It has worked well as long as we bring food!

Stop the pity party

Whenever a group of spouses get together, it's often only a mat-ter of time before the pity party starts. Make it a habit to view things in a positive manner rather than complaining and sound-ing ungrateful for all the things we have so freely.

> Once our minds are "tattooed" with negative thinking, our chances for long-term success diminish.—**John Maxwell**

I'm ashamed of how easily I get caught up in the pity party. When a pity party starts (and it will), try to input positive com-ments into the conversation. Things will quickly look brighter for everyone.

SOLUTIONS

I am by no means claiming to know the answers to the many leadership issues. However, a few practices I have observed seem to work well and I gladly pass them on to you.

Issues of no one showing up

Instead of conducting meetings every month with only your particular group of spouses, move up to the next level and conduct meetings on a larger scale. For example, if the battalion/ battery or a group made up of several companies would plan for each of the companies/groups to host an event for the entire larger group, more people would show up. An event could be "Alpha Company" hosting a dress swap the month before the military ball. Alpha Company would be the host, but all the other companies (B, C, D, etc.) would pitch in and help out with food, drinks, and so forth. Then the next quarter perhaps B Company could host an event and bring in a guest speaker on a "hot topic" while the other companies pitch in with food, drinks, and so on.

This gives each company an opportunity to host an event on a larger scale and also gives the leadership in the other companies a break from trying to plan an event every month. In essence, within one year, each company will have to host only one big event. The individual companies can still have meetings within their small group, but most like having a larger event with more attendance. Each company will learn from each other and it's a great way to meet many spouses from other companies you may never have met.

Finding leadership

Leadership must start from the top. If the commander isn't interested in or doesn't take time for the family programs, the leadership will most likely suffer. Instead of having only the senior spouse or someone being "volunTOLD" as the "default leader," have spouses submit a simple application to become the leader. Have the group elect a leader to serve a one-year term. This way, people who actually desire and have a passion to lead may become the leader. The senior spouse could serve as an advisor to the elected leader. If junior spouses knew they would have the guidance and advice if needed, more would probably step up and serve in a leadership role. Again, this will have to come from the command.

A one-year term is doable without causing burnout. This type of leadership is currently occurring in a "Special Operations" unit and is working very well. This could be a model for all of us to adopt.

Paid positions are also having a positive impact for the volunteer leadership. Having a paid family programs position is taking much of the weight off the volunteers. This program is still being fine-tuned, as with any new program, and it will take time to perfect it.

For leaders who are attempting to lead and have no desire to do so, it shows. Most of us can pick up the vibes and we know if you are leading out of care and concern or the pressure of whom you may be married to. There is no shame in not wanting to lead if it's not your passion. Believe me, the spouses in the unit would much rather have a leader who wants to be in the leadership position than someone who is only doing a bare minimum job. It hinders the entire growth and effectiveness of the support group. Don't just keep the title of "leader" and not do anything! Appoint someone else who wants to do the job. We deserve quality, effective leadership!

If you want to lead, don't worry about what you don't know. According to John Maxwell (#1 leadership expert), "People do not care how much you know until they know how much you care." Lead from your heart and you won't go wrong. There will be time for training, and other passionate spouses are there to help you if you only ask for their assistance. Put all pride on the back burner and just be your loving humble self! People are so hungry for caring, motivated, passionate leadership. If you can bring that to the table, you will be a success in any group.

Personality conflicts

You and I both know there are people we would rather not be around. We need to look at these types of people as "testers." It's easy to lead a group of loving, caring, fun spouses. But what about the loudmouths, the critical ones, the snobby, proud, and arrogant ones who wear their service member's rank? We all have them.

They are our test of whether we are true leaders or not. We have to learn to get over it! People are people and in every group in society you have the loudmouths, the critical, the snobby, the proud, and so forth. This is the world we live in and the sooner we learn to function in and around these "thorns" the better off we'll be. You can't let someone else's shortcomings rob you of being part of a greater good. Take a few moments and think about the "thorns" in your group. Are they happy people, loving people, nice people? Are their marriages working, and are they happy in their jobs or life in general? Probably not. If you take time to ask why some people behave in such an ugly way, you may soon realize their life is not so rosy and they are most likely miserable in one way or another. It's been stated, "Hurting people will hurt people." Look beyond the thorns and you may see a hurting person needing your leadership or care more than the easy, happy, nice spouses in your group.

One book that has helped me in dealing with the "thorns" in my life is *Fool-Proofing Your Life: An Honorable Way to Deal with the Impossible People In Your Life* by Jan Silvious. This book saved me from going completely insane during one particular tour. You do not have to be in a leadership role for this book to help you deal with your "thorns." Every leader should have this book by his or her bed.

> Theodore Roosevelt puts it best: "Do what you can, with what you have, where you are."

As long as we can go to sleep each night knowing we have done our best, that's really all that matters. You cannot control how other people act or what they say. Worry about your actions and what's coming out of your mouth and it will all work out. Be the best *you* can be, and live your life in a manner worth mirroring and stop fretting about what other people are doing or not doing.

Don't use lack of leadership as an excuse to hinder your life. Take control, become proactive, and get out there and make a difference. You count and you have gifts and talents that others could benefit from. We are all leaders in some way or another. Lead your own life and then reach out to help others.

> Destiny is not a matter of chance, it is a matter of choice; it is not a thing to be waited for, it is a thing to be achieved.
> **—Winston Churchill**

POEMS

I WROTE the following poems from my continuing experience as a military wife. The reader who is not in the military will get a quick picture of who the people are who make the military their life, how they live through the pain of loss, how they cope with their loved ones away, and what makes a military wife and who she is. Those who are in the military and read them, I hope will gain from having me express their lifestyle for them so that they can see they are not alone and others are in the same circumstances. Many have read these poems and said, "Yes, that's me. How did she know?" They will weep, and that is good too. Each poem has a special meaning for a specific time and place. I hope you benefit from them.

This poem is dedicated to our fallen heroes. I wrote it after my close friend Christina's husband died. You could read this poem at any military funeral or memorial.

Warriors of Freedom

Today tears fell on my old worn beret,
As I see another Warrior has completed his stay.

His mission is now complete, he's come forth as gold,
His memory gives us strength, while we travel down this road.

I see the young widow, trembling so with grief,
The children there beside her, all in disbelief.

Another dawn will rise, another mission to complete,
Freedom is never free, destiny we shall meet.

We are the keepers, of freedom and liberty,
We'll be strong and courageous, for America always free.

Tears have fallen, on my old worn beret,[1]
For a friend, a soldier,[2] a hero, we remember here today.

★   ★   ★

The next poem was written to depict the strength and courage of military spouses.

---

1. For the words *worn beret*, you may substitute *red, green, brown,* or *black beret,* as appropriate.
2. You may substitute any service member (*marine, airman,* etc.) for the word *soldier*.

A *Military Wife*

A military wife
Her virtues are rare
She's a pillar of strength
She's his breath of fresh air

Her sacrifices are many
As she answers his call
She looks fear in the face
She's the bravest of all

She's self-sufficient and flexible
More patriotic than most
Her pride is contagious
But seldom does she boast

She's a mommy, a daddy
A banker, and a nurse,
She's the hundred-mile-an-hour tape[3]
She keeps money in her purse

She's part of a sisterhood
That time will never fade
She's been known to call angels
To act as his aid

This wife has a mission
That few would accept
She's the wind beneath his wings
Courage must be kept

A military wife[4]
An honor indeed
For her warrior is the keeper
Of freedom and liberty

3. Duct tape.
4. You may substitute *wife* with *spouse* and *military* with *ranger, special forces, night stalker, marine, air force, navy,* etc.

This poem depicts the life of the military spouse.

Far Away

Oh my loved one so far away,
How I needed you at home today.
Johnny's been crying for two weeks straight,
Jane at fifteen went on her first date.

The van needs fixing, but money is tight,
Come next payday, it will be all right.
Angry words from the past have all been erased,
If only I could hold you, and feel your embrace.

Some days are better, but the nights seem so long,
In the corner of my mind, so many things can go wrong.
I must stand on my faith, day after day,
That my prayers will be answered, and all is okay.

How I long for our love, to be together at last,
I'll wait for you patiently, for these dark days to pass.
When we meet again, our love will have grown,
With each deployment, we add strength that's unknown.

Oh my loved one so far away,
How I long for you here today.

RESOURCES AND SUPPORT GROUPS

MILITARY SERVICE MEMBERS and their spouses often overlook numerous resources and support agencies dedicated to assisting families. Being a military family is a challenge, and no one will disagree with that, but one thing is for sure—you are not alone.

The particular branch of service you are affiliated with will determine what support group is best for you. Every unit should have an established family support or readiness group. As you read this, many of you may be moaning over a bad experience with one of these support groups. Most of us at one time or another have probably had at least one negative experience within a support group.

Take a few moments and think of all the groups, whether military or civilian, you've been involved with during your life, including your workplace, church, sports team, and so on. I'm sure you encounter people or policies within all these groups that you disagree with. Don't allow a particular person or policy to take anything away from what the group has to offer. Not all support groups are alike, and as members of a group change, the dynamics of the group change. The mission of the group is the most important thing.

Most unit support groups have volunteers who, for the most part, lead the group and genuinely care and devote enormous amounts of time and effort to make the group a success. One or two personalities are bound to clash in any group setting. Like all the other clubs or groups you may be a part of, this clash should not stop you from participating or benefiting from the group. You can't benefit at all, if you don't participate. Make yourself part of the solution.

Support groups are a great way to develop friendships, share information, and learn about community services. If you're not plugged into a support group, you're missing a huge benefit for military families. Most families who stay involved with their unit's support group are better equipped to handle the challenges of separation due to deployments. When the deployments come, many of the spouses have already developed a solid foundation of friends and knowledge of the resources available to them. If your particular unit support group is not for you, I encourage you to seek out a support group elsewhere, such as a community spouses club, an on-line spouses club, or a church group.

Those of us who have been involved with the military for several years have a responsibility to share our wealth of personal experiences with the younger spouses of the unit. We should never forget the days when we struggled with not knowing the ropes, fear of the unknown, and barely having enough money to get by. Even we seasoned spouses still encounter these uneasy feelings, but most of us have learned where to get the support we need and have developed a network of military friendships. You have nothing to lose and everything to gain by being involved.

> Everyone has something to offer a group. It's not about what you can get. It's about what you give that makes a positive difference. Make a difference!

In addition to support groups, I hope you will learn from this book to remember to communicate, listen, stick to routines but take care of yourself and the kids, keep a sharp eye on the finances, and love and support your service member. You can be successful at home with the kids or have a successful career as a military spouse with at-home work or outside work, and your family life can stay *normal* with some adjustments to a situation that is not. No matter what, stay positive and hold on to your faith.

The following websites and books are only a fraction of what's available about military life. They are here as a starting point. Be proactive and continue to embrace and learn the many wonderful facets of being a military spouse. Hooah!

MUST-HAVE WEBSITES FOR LIFE IN THE MILITARY
Many of these sites should be your first place for research

Service websites

Each site is full of helpful resources and links to numerous other military-related sites.

www.navy.mil   U.S. Navy.

www.army.mil   U.S. Army.

www.af.mil   U.S. Air Force.

www.usmc.mil   U.S. Marine Corps.

www.uscg.mil/uscg.shtm   U.S. Coast Guard.

www.defenselink.mil/news   Pentagon News.

www.militaryonesource.com This website is the MacDaddy military website. If offers anything and everything you will need and then some. All calls are answered live by master's-level trained consultants.

Military OneSource: 1-800-342-9647
Collect from outside the United States: 1-484-530-5908

www.military.com   This site covers all services, providing information for education, money, careers, news, shopping, etc.

www.nmfa.org   The National Military Family Association educates and improves the quality of military life. Tons of information on various topics.

www.militaryhomefront.dod.mil   Department of Defense website for official military community and family policy program information.

www.milspouse.com   *Military Spouse* is the first magazine dedicated to all military spouses. A magazine for spouses by spouses.

www.themilitarycoalition.org   Comprises thirty-four organizations representing 5.5 million members of the uniformed services: active, reserve, retired, survivors, veterans, and their families.

www.operationhomefront.net   Emergency assistance and morale to military service members and their families left behind, and "wounded warriors" when they return home.

www.netpets.org   The *MilitaryPets*FOSTER Project. "A NationWide & Global network of Individual Foster Homes that will house, nurture and care for the dogs, cats, birds, horses and all other pets for all the Military personnel *Only*. *(Foster: to give temporary nurture, care and shelter.)*"

Great websites to plan a getaway while your service member is deployed or for midtour R&R (rest and relaxation) and/or homecoming

www.afvclub.com   Armed Forces Vacation Club. A "space available" program for affordable condominium vacations worldwide. A must!

www.armymwr.com   Army morale, welfare, and recreation site, including lodging at Army posts.

www.dodlodging.net   Lodging at Air Force and Naval bases.

www.uscg.mil/mwr/lodging/lodging.asp   Coast Guard lodging locations.

www.usms-mccs.org   Recreation lodging on Marine Corps installations.

> Did you know as an active duty service member/family member or retiree you have access to any and all Armed Forces lodging and recreation facilities? The opportunities for fun and vacation are endless and affordable! Check them out and plan your next getaway.

CHAPTER 1:

DEPARTURE AND THE GAMES WE PLAY

www.hooah4health.com   Don't let the name fool you. This site can benefit all members in all services, not only the Army. It offers updated articles on the emotional cycle of deployments. Mind, body, spirit, environment awareness, mental health self-assessment program, etc.

CHAPTER 2: COMMUNICATION

www.dalecarnegie.com   Learn key communication skills from the freely downloadable booklet.

Book

Chapman, Gary. *The Five Love Languages.* Teaches and explains how to communicate your love to each other. Also in children's, teens', singles', and group formats.

CHAPTER 3: FINANCIAL HARDSHIP

www.dfas.mil   Defense Finance and Accounting Service. Sign up for "The Department of Defense Savings Deposit Program" (SDP). It provides a high interest rate on savings for deployed service members.

www.daveramsey.com   *Financial Peace University* is an intensive training course for personal finance. FPU helps military members strategically and effectively remove debt and build wealth.

www.militarymoney.com   *Military Money* is a magazine that offers a vast assortment of financial readiness for the military and various other aspects of military life.

In case you have the urge to splurge or shop using your military benefits and savings

www.commissaries.com   Defense commissary. It's worth the trip. Coupons, promotions, diet tips, food alerts and recalls, etc.

www.aafes.com   Army and Air Force exchange. No tax and shipping is included in purchase price.

www.navy-nex.com   Navy exchange.

www.usmc-mccs.org/shopping   Marine Corps exchange.

(See p. 212 for additional financial websites.)

CHAPTER 4: INFIDELITY

www.dailystrength.org/groups/infidelity-in-the-military   This group is for military members and spouses (past and present) who have dealt with infidelity in their marriage or relationship.

CHAPTER 5: CHILDREN

www.MilitaryChild.org   Military Child Education Coalition. Network of military installations and school districts.

www.sesameworkshop.org   Sesame Workshop. Innovative and engaging educational content.

www.zerotothree.org   Zero to Three offers ways to help military families support their young children during the stress of separations, deployments, and relocations.

www.operationgiveahug.org   The goal of Operation Give a Hug is to give dolls to military children throughout the world who are missing Mom or Dad during the long deployments.

CHAPTER 6: CAREER

www.milspouse.org   Military Spouse resource library for "employment, education, and relocation information."

www.msccn.org   Military Spouse Corporate Career Network (MSCCN). Created and operated by military spouses.

www.militaryspousejobsearch.org Military Spouse Job Search. This website is designed for military spouses. There is a "New Jobs" meter so you can see the latest jobs available.

www.militaryonesource.com. Military Spouse Career Advancement Account Program. This program provides resources and funds (several thousands of dollars) for spouses who desire a portable career. This program may be accessed through Military OneSource.

CHAPTER 7: HOME FRIES

www.armywifenetwork.com Complete online/live talk show and support group founded and operated by military spouses for military spouses of all branches. A must-have during deployments.

www.cinchouse.com CinCHouse, pronounced "sink-house" provides "information, resources, and a community of friends to help you survive the toughest times and enjoy the adventures of military life."

www.ahrn.com The Automated Housing Referral Network is sponsored by the Department of Defense and is designed to improve the process of securing available housing for relocating military members and their families. Free service to sell your home or buy a home.

CHAPTER 8: HOMECOMING

Sites for planning a homecoming getaway

www.afvclub.com Armed Forces vacation club that offers condominium rentals at resorts around the world for a deep-discounted price for military service members.

www.usmc-mccs.org/lodging   Marine Corps lodging.

www.armymwr.com/travel/lodging/default.aspx   Army lodging.

www.dodlodging.net   Air Force and Navy lodging.

www.uscg.mil/mwr/lodging/lodging.asp   Coast Guard lodging.

www.nps.gov   National parks locations.

All service members and their authorized family members have access to all Armed Forces lodging and recreation facilities, campgrounds, RV parks, etc.

CHAPTER 9: WOUNDED WARRIORS = WOUNDED FAMILIES

www.woundedwarriorproject.com This site states:

The mission of the Wounded Warrior Project is to *honor and empower wounded warriors.*

Purpose:

- To raise awareness and enlist the public's aid for the needs of severely injured service men and women,
- To help severely injured service members aid and assist each other, and
- To provide unique, direct programs and services to meet the needs of severely injured service members.

---

www.notalone.org   It's hard to know what normal is. Not Alone is a community of your peers sharing stories of reclaiming their lives after war. Here, you'll listen to others who live the war after the war. You'll find people who understand what you're going through.

www.fisherhouse.org   "Supporting America's military in their time of need, we provide *a home away from home*' that enables family members to be close to a loved one at the most stressful time—during hospitalization for an illness, disease or injury."

www.ncptsd.va.gov   National Center for PTSD (Post-Traumatic Stress Disorder). Veteran's Affairs site for recognition and treatment of PTSD and other stress-related disorders.

CHAPTER 10: PRAYER

www.cmf.com   Christian Military Fellowship. Support through Bible studies, articles, training, leadership, etc.

excellentorpraiseworthy.org   An online devotional to help military families stay connected during deployments.

jocelyngreen.wordpress.com   Resources and spiritual encouragement for the unsung heroes at home. Christian Military Wife Resources and websites.

www.mil.min.com   Lots of links for military members and families. Homecoming ideas, deployments, spouses, prayer guide, and more.

www.oneplace.com   The leading provider of Christian audio content on the Internet. Here's what that means for you: Listen to your favorite Christian broadcasters (such as Dr. R. C. Sproul, Chuck Swindoll, Kay Arthur, Charles Stanley, and Chuck Colson) anytime, at your convenience!

www.judaism.com   Your guide to Judaism. Articles, resources, recipes, history, books, and more.

www.islam.com   Articles, education, calendar, history, and more.

CHAPTER 11: DECISIONS WE NEVER WANT TO MAKE

www.cem.va.gov   National Cemetery Administration. Information on the VA's national cemeteries and other burial benefits.

www.arlingtoncemetery.org   Arlington Cemetery. Information on military funerals, ceremonies, and The Tomb of the Unknowns.

www.taps.org   Tragedy Assistance Program for Survivors (TAPS). National veteran's service organization that provides compassionate care through peer-based emotional support, grief, and trauma resources; seminars; case work assistance; and 24/7 crisis intervention to all those who have been affected by death in the Armed Forces. Toll-free: 800-959-TAPS (8277).

www.goldstarwives.org   An organization of military wives and husbands whose spouse died while on active duty or from service-connected disabilities.

Book

Steen, Joanne M., and M. Regina Asaro. *Military Widow: A Survival Guide.* A first-of-its-kind survival guide for widows of service personnel that tackles the unique and complex issues arising from the death of a spouse in the military.

CHAPTER 12: LEADERSHIP

www.carlisle.army.mil/usawc/dclm/joint.htm   Complete website links to Military Family Programs for senior spouses from all branches.

www.johnmaxwell.com   John Maxwell is an internationally recognized leadership expert, speaker, and author. His book sales exceed 18 million copies. EQUIP, an organization he founded, has trained more than 5 million leaders worldwide. Every year he speaks to audiences as diverse as Fortune 500 companies, international government leaders, and the United States Military Academy at West Point.

www.stephencovey.com   Stephen Covey is respected worldwide as a leadership authority, family expert, teacher, organizational consultant, and author. His advice has helped countless individuals.

Book

Silvious, Jan. *Fool-Proofing Your Life: An Honorable Way to Deal with the Impossible People In Your Life.* A must for any leader.

Additional financial websites

www.irs.gov   Especially the Armed Forces Tax Guide, Latest Publication.

www.dfas.mil/army2/militarypay/requestingyourles/army_ reading_your_les.pdf   This will show you how to read an LES (Leave and Earning Statement).

tsp.gov   Thrift Savings Plan; an alternate retirement savings vehicle for service members. Contribution limits vary year to year.

www.bbb.org   Check out that company before you do business.

www.annualcreditreport.com/cra/index.jsp   View your credit report free once per year from each of the major credit bureaus—Experian, Equifax, and TransUnion.

INDEX

ABOUT THE AUTHOR

SHELLIE VANDEVOORDE is a military veteran who served her country for six years and continues to be a devoted army wife and mother. During her army career she worked in the communications field. She also completed airborne and air-assault training. Shellie met her husband while in the army.

After Shellie left the army, she attended the police academy in Fayetteville, North Carolina, and became a deputy sheriff. She was assigned to street patrol, undercover narcotics, community policing, and hostage negotiating and later became a detective.

After moving to Savannah, Georgia, Shellie wrote her book, *Separated by Duty, United in Love.*

Shellie is an active volunteer at a number of organizations. At family readiness, she is a certified instructor for family team building and involved in company, battalion, and division leadership committees. She continues ongoing family support training and attends conventions within the military.

Shellie has been a guest speaker for National Women's History Month as well as the United States Special Operations Family Readiness Conference. She has received several volunteer awards including the Outstanding Civilian Service Award from the United States Army.

As a military spouse, a working mother, a volunteer, and one who has lived in a long-distance relationship, Shellie offers a no-nonsense guide to getting the most out of your relationship. Sharing her experiences as well as those of hundreds of others who have survived long-distance relationships, Shellie continues to serve the people of this great nation with this book. You can contact her at www.Separatedbyduty.com.